EAGLES
FACTS AND TRIVIA

EAGLES
FACTS AND TRIVIA

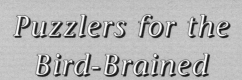

*Puzzlers for the
Bird-Brained*

by John Maxymuk

Camino Books, Inc.
Philadelphia

Manufactured in the United States of America

1 2 3 4 5 09 08 07

Library of Congress Cataloging-in-Publication Data

Maxymuk, John.
  Eagles facts and trivia : puzzlers for the bird-brained / by John
Maxymuk.
     p. cm.
  ISBN-13: 978-1-933822-04-4 (alk. paper)
  ISBN-10: 1-933822-04-X (alk. paper)
  1. Philadelphia Eagles (Football team)--Miscellanea. I. Title.

GV956.P44M393 2006
796.332'640974811--dc22   2006021447

Cover and interior design: Jan Greenberg

This book is available at a special discount on bulk purchases
for promotional, business, and educational use.

Publisher
Camino Books, Inc.
P.O. Box 59026
Philadelphia, PA 19102

www.caminobooks.com

This book is dedicated to

the usual suspects:

Suzanne, Katie and Juliane.

Contents

Preface

When I began writing *Eagles by the Numbers: Jersey Numbers and the Players Who Wore Them*, there was no history of the Philadelphia Eagles, so I attempted to fill the void. Similarly, there has been no Eagles trivia book up till now—hence, the book you are holding in your hands.

The Eagles are one of the oldest teams in the NFL and have a fascinating past. They've had owners who went bankrupt and ones who were awash in money. They've cancelled games because of threatening weather and a threatening playing surface. They have made great trades, horrible trades, draft-day trades and even a complex franchise trade. Their drafts have produced stars and starters as well as draft busts and police busts. They've had quarterbacks who gave 'em hell and quarterbacks from hell. Their fans who once were hampered by Blue Laws were later handcuffed by a city courtroom in their home stadium. We have seen fistfights on the field, fistfights off the field and fistfights in the stands, hard hits given and hard hits received in each case. Eagle fans have booed underachievers, mediocrities, struggling Hall of Famers and beloved cultural figures and cheered touchdowns, goal line stands and injuries to despised opponents. We have watched thrilling games when the Eagles stole victory from the jaws of defeat and devastating ones when the Birds tore defeat from the embrace of victory.

One can't argue that there hasn't been a lot of bad football in Philadelphia over the years. A small girl came up to a display of Eagle photos I had set up to promote my previous book at a local book fair and was identifying all the recent players. I said to her father that she sounded like an Eagle fan, and he replied that she loved the team. After she left, I turned to a friend and said, "She has no idea what she's in for." Eagle fans need to be hearty souls. In 2005, the Eagles went 6-10, a winning percentage of .375. In Philadelphia's 73 seasons up to that point, they produced 30 seasons at or below .375. They have had 38 losing seasons—more losing years than winning ones. Yet, recent decades have been more positive. Since 1978, Philadelphia has had 17 winning seasons and just 11 losing ones. The new millennium under Andy Reid will be remembered as the team's second glory years (after the 1940s) if they can manage to win a Super Bowl or two.

Above all else, the Eagles are a storyteller's team and a joy to write about. They have been populated by some of the quirkiest and most colorful players, coaches and management in all of pro football history. These characters have taken part in some of the strangest, funniest, wildest and most disturbing events in the lore of football. Through it all, certain common character traits continually emerge in both good and bad Eagle teams. Eagles make themselves known; they are not shy and retiring. That's one thing the Eagles have in common with their fans—they will not go quietly, and you will know they are here, win or lose.

I have tried to have some fun mining nuggets from the rich past of the Eagles and making fresh connections to entertain and inform readers. While this is a book of trivia, I have tried to avoid trivial questions. In other words, I strove to steer clear of statistics and stories that tell you nothing of any great significance. I think that the best questions are those that require some explanation and context to give a better understanding of the nature of the team, its players and fans.

The structure of the book is 60 theme-oriented quizzes of 10 questions each. Why 60? Well, there are 60 minutes in a football game, to start. More than that, 60 takes on special resonance in Philadelphia where the Eagles' last championship came in 1960, powered by the player for whom 60 is now retired by the franchise, Chuck Bednarik. Bednarik takes it deeper still, being known as the "60-Minute Man" for playing the entire 1960 championship game on both offense and defense. Did I mention that Chuck wore 60 for 60 minutes to lead the Eagles to the 1960 title? So 60 quizzes it is then. Let's just hope we don't have to wait 60 years to see the next championship.

The quizzes are arranged in six different sections: History, Glory and Rivalries, Players and Positions, Management, the Offbeat, and Records. Each quiz has an additional Overtime question that is based on the uniform number that corresponds with the number of the quiz. That's 660 questions in all, not to mention that several questions involve multiple parts. If any reader gets more than four or five questions wrong, I would recommend a crash course in Eagle history via *Eagles by the Numbers* by an author near and dear to my heart and wallet. My wish with this book is that Eagle fans find it fun and informative. Now, on to the questions.

Introduction

On a slow September day in 1986, I was searching through my desk at the *Philadelphia Daily News*, looking for a column idea. I found a copy of the *Dallas Cowboys Weekly* and saw an ad that read: "The Dallas Cowboys Trivia Game. It's fun for family, friends and die-hard Cowboys fans. Over 2,400 questions. Order now."

I knew I had my column. If the Dallas Cowboys could have a trivia game, why not the Philadelphia Eagles? Besides, it made more sense for the Eagles. They had not won an NFL championship in more than a quarter of a century. They were on their way to their fifth consecutive losing season. When it came to being trivial on a year-in, year-out basis, I'd put the Eagles up against anybody.

So I wrote down 40 questions — some serious, some frivolous — and put them in the form of a column. I didn't spend a lot of time on research. Mostly, I just plucked a few tidbits off the top of my head. Here are a few samples:

By winning the final game of the 1985 season, Fred Bruney became the second undefeated head coach in Eagles history. The other, at 2-0, is (a) Bert Bell, (b) Wayne Millner, (c) Bo McMillin.

What rock group invited kicker Tony Franklin on stage during a 1981 Spectrum concert? (a) the Eagles, (b) Devo, (c) Kool and the Gang.

What does wide receiver Scott Fitzkee have tattooed on his lower leg? (a) a Nittany Lion, (b) a grasshopper, (c) a pass pattern.

(The correct answers, just in case you are wondering, are "c," "a" and "b.")

I also tossed in a bonus question: How many former Eagles can you name with last names that begin with the letter "I"? Each correct answer was worth two points. At the time, there were only three: James Ignatius, a guard who played in 1935; Ed Illman, a back who was on the original team in 1933 and Willie Irvin, a back who played in 1953.

The *Daily News* ran the column the next day and the strangest thing happened. I began receiving phone calls and letters from people who loved the quiz and wanted me to do a second one. So I did.

Again, the questions ranged from arcane to just plain dumb.

Who was the Eagles trainer before Otho Davis? (a) Moose Detty, (b) Moose Dupont, (c) Bullwinkle Moose.

What size shoe does defensive end Dennis "Big Foot" Harrison wear? (a) 15, (b) 16, (c) 17 EEE.

Punter Merritt Kersey is best remembered for his pet (a) boa constrictor, (b) skunk, (c) armadillo.

(The answer for each of these questions was "a.")

Once again, there was an amazing response. People really enjoyed the quiz. It jogged their memories, it made them laugh, and it brightened what proved to be a miserable 5-10-1 season, the team's first under head coach Buddy Ryan.

I'll always remember one particular phone call. The man was in his 30s, a life-long Eagles fan who started going to the games at Franklin Field with his father. He said his father was undergoing cancer treatments and the trivia quizzes helped them pass the time in the hospital.

"It's the only time I've seen him smile," the man said. He thanked me.

"No, thank you," I said.

So I suppose it was inevitable that someone would take this idea and turn it into a book. Clearly, the fans are interested and John Maxymuk is well-equipped to do the honors. In 2006, John published a book entitled *Eagles by the Numbers*, tracing the history of the team through its jersey numbers, from Tony Franklin (1) to Jerome Brown (99) and hitting every Dave Smukler (13) and Augie Lio (62) in between.

There was a lot of information in that book that might be considered trivia—for example, did you know that Mario Giannelli, a guard who played on the championship teams of 1948 and '49, was nicknamed "Yo Yo"?—except for the fact that to a true Eagles fan nothing about the team is trivial. Eagles history is something the people of this city live and breathe every day. Most of all, they love revisiting that history and *Eagles Facts and Trivia* will allow them to enjoy it to the max.

SECTION I

HISTORY

EAGLE PREHISTORY

THE PHILADELPHIA EAGLES are not our town's first professional football team. Professional football in the City of Brotherly Love dates back to the very beginning of the 20th century, although on a very limited scale before the 1920s. The main forerunner to the Eagles was the Frankford Yellow Jackets who represented the Frankford Athletic Association for roughly 20 years, beginning as an independent club in 1912 before joining the NFL in 1924. However, there were other professional teams that called Philadelphia home prior to the Eagles' arrival in 1933.

1. What prominent figure from major league baseball formed one of the first professional football teams in Philadelphia?

2. During the course of their eight years in the NFL, the Frankford Yellow Jackets played on average 16 games per year, more than any other team. Why?

3. One of the biggest stars of the NBA in the 1980s and 1990s was the grandson of one of the biggest stars on the Yellow Jackets. Can you name them?

4. The Yellow Jackets had a star punt returner who was only 5'5" and 145 pounds. He played "quarterback," that is blocking back, in Frankford's Single Wing Offense. Who was he?

5. The one Frankford player who is in the Pro Football Hall of Fame was an end who also was their coach for that championship season. Who was he?

6. In 2003, Governor Ed Rendell got involved in an appeal by the nearby city of Pottsville for the NFL to recognize the Pottsville Maroons rather than the Chicago Cardinals as the official champions of the 1925 season. What part did the Yellow Jackets play in the 80-year-old controversy?

7. In 1926, Red Grange formed his own American Football League to compete with the NFL, and Philadelphia had an entry called the Quakers. What was significant about the two Philadelphia football teams that year?

8. Who was the only player to play for the Frankford Yellow Jackets, Pottsville Maroons and Philadelphia Eagles?

9. In 1922, the Frankford Athletic Association built a stadium for the Yellow Jackets. Until Lincoln Financial Field opened in 2003, it was

the only Philadelphia stadium devoted solely to a professional football team. What happened to it?

10. Frankford ceased operations after the 1931 season; the Eagles began in 1933. Are the Philadelphia Eagles a continuation of the Frankford Yellow Jackets?

 OVERTIME: *Uniform Number Question:* Although number 1 was worn several times by Frankford, it wasn't worn by an Eagle until the team's 39th season. Who was the cheerful fellow who wore number 1 in 1971?

TRIVIA QUIZ 2

THE 1930s

LOCAL BLUEBLOOD BERT BELL led a group of investors who purchased a new NFL franchise to represent Philadelphia in 1933. The team was named the Eagles in honor of the symbol for President Roosevelt's National Recovery Administration that also began that year. The Eagles' original colors were blue and yellow, and they were a scuffling outfit right from the start. For the decade of the 1930s, the Birds finished 18-55-3, a winning percentage of just .257.

1. Who did the Eagles play in their very first game and who won?

2. Who scored first for Philadelphia?

3. Who was the first coach of the team?

4. When did the Eagles win their first game?

5. The Eagles tied the Bears 3-3 on Sunday, November 12, 1933. Why was this game a first for Philadelphia?

6. In 1939, Bert Bell postponed the opening game due to "threatening weather." What was the real reason?

7. In their second season, the Eagles posted their largest margin of victory ever. Against whom?

8. In 1936, the Eagles only scored 51 points in 12 games. Who was their leading scorer and with how many points?

9. In 1939, the 0-3-1 Eagles and the 2-2-1 Brooklyn Dodgers played an immensely significant game. Why?

10. On November 26, 1933, the Eagles record was 3-3-1. Why is that memorable?

 OVERTIME: *Uniform Number Question:* In the past decade, Luther Broughton became the second player to wear four numbers for the Birds. The first played in the 1930s and one of the numbers he wore was 2. Who was he?

=====TRIVIA QUIZ=====

THE 1940s

ALTHOUGH THE DECADE STARTED with a 1-10 season in 1940, the 1940s turned out to be the original glory days for the franchise. In the last six seasons of the 1940s, the team finished second in the division three times and then went to the title game the next three years, winning it all twice. Their record for the decade was 58-47-5 and for the last six seasons was 48-26-3. They went 3-1 in the postseason for the decade.

1. In 1940, the last year of the Bert Bell regime, the Eagles did something offensively that they had never done before and wouldn't do again for many seasons. What was it?

2. How did Lex Thompson become the owner of the Eagles?

3. In the dealings between Pittsburgh and Philadelphia in 1941, did the Eagles acquire anyone of lasting importance?

4. What was the first thing Greasy Neale changed about the offense in 1941?

5. What concession to World War II did the Eagles make in 1943?

6. When was the Eagles' first winning season?

7. In 1948, the Eagles beat the Giants, Redskins and Boston Yanks by identical scores. What was that score?

8. What was the alignment for Greasy Neale's "Eagle Defense"?

9. What tragedy occurred immediately after the 1948 opening game loss to the champion Cardinals?

10. Who scored the most points for the Eagles in the 1940s?

OVERTIME: *Uniform Number Question:* The back who threw the first TD pass in Eagles history wore 3 for part of his career. Who was he?

TRIVIA QUIZ 4

THE 1950s

THE GLORY DAYS FADED QUICKLY for the Eagles in the 1950s. What remained from the rough bunch of war veterans who dominated the NFL in the immediate postwar years was their roughness and belligerency. The 1950s Eagles took a back seat to no one in toughness during this sometimes brutal decade of pro football. Unfortunately, they had more head coaches than winning seasons in the 1950s—six coaches, four winning seasons and a 51-64-5 record for the period.

1. The opening game of the 1950 season is sometimes referred to as the "First Super Bowl." Why?
2. What Eagle played in every game but one during this decade?
3. Who scored the most points for the Eagles in the 1950s?
4. What two backs were the first black Eagles?
5. Who was the first Latino Eagle?
6. Who had a two-game tenure as head coach?
7. What did Hugh Devore and Buck Shaw have in common?
8. To whom did the Eagles originally offer the head coaching job in 1958?
9. How did Commissioner Bert Bell convince Norm Van Brocklin to accept a trade to the Eagles in 1958?
10. In 1957, the Eagles drafted an entire starting backfield. Who were the players and in what round were they picked?

 OVERTIME: *Uniform Number Question:* 4 was worn by one kicker in the Buddy Ryan era for only one game. Who was he and why the quick exit?

THE 1960s

THE 1960s STARTED WITH the Eagles' most recent championship and went downhill from there. After the magical championship season of 1960, the Eagles only managed two more winning years throughout the decade, and in one of those, 1966, they were actually outscored by their opponents. Under the coaching mastery of Nick Skorich, Joe Kuharich and Jerry Williams, Philadelphia went 57-76-5 in the 1960s.

1. How was the opening game of the 1960s similar to the opening game of the 1950s?
2. Injuries played a major role in the early part of the decade. Whose injury helped burnish Chuck Bednarik's legend in 1960?
3. What two receivers suffered broken arms in 1962?
4. The first major injury of the 1962 season happened at the end of 1961. Who got hurt?
5. Who was the coach credited with making a star out of Sonny Jurgensen?
6. The Eagles beat Dallas 24-21 in 1966 with all three touchdowns coming in an unusual way. How did they score?
7. What was special about Bobby Shann's very short career?
8. What season did the Eagles screw up in reverse by having a winning streak?
9. Who was the first former Eagle player to coach the team?
10. The Pro Football Hall of Fame opened in 1963. Who was the only charter member from the Eagles?

 OVERTIME: *Uniform Number Question:* Who was the first Eagle quarterback to wear 5?

TRIVIA QUIZ 6

THE 1970s

THE 1970s WERE THE OPPOSITE of the 1960s—the Eagles started out awful, but became a top-flight team by the end of the decade. It was a decade in which the total mismanagement was best exemplified by the team trading away all its first- and second-round draft picks for a five-year period. Despite the bleak outlook mid-decade, hope was restored through the undying efforts of Dick Vermeil. Vermeil's work could not erase the reality of that awful past, however, and Philadelphia went 56-84-4 for the 1970s.

1. At whom did Jerry Williams lash out in 1971?
2. What controversial new policy did Ed Khayat enact upon becoming coach?
3. What was the unique thing about the 1972 holdout by Bill Bradley and Tim Rossovich?
4. Who was in the "Fire High Gang"?
5. Although Mike McCormack had played under Paul Brown and coached under Vince Lombardi, what other coach did he try to emulate?
6. What happened to Howard Cosell the first time he came to Philadelphia to broadcast a *Monday Night Football* game?
7. What unheralded guard played the most games of any Eagle for the decade?
8. What is Fred Hill's lasting legacy in Philadelphia?
9. What was the most consequential booing incident in team history?
10. How many times did Philadelphia beat Dallas in this decade?

 OVERTIME: *Uniform Number Question:* What backup quarterback who wore 6 followed Rich Kotite to the Jets?

TRIVIA QUIZ 7

THE 1980s

A DECADE BEGINNING UNDER DICK VERMEIL and ending under Buddy Ryan is bound to be interesting and at least somewhat successful. Despite the dreadful Marion Campbell years in the middle of the period, the Eagles achieved their first winning decade since the 1940s, going 76-74-2. They made the playoffs four times, the Super Bowl once, and went 2-4 in the postseason.

1. Dick Vermeil brought in a veteran West Coast coach to work with Ron Jaworski in 1979. Who was he?
2. The most serious union work action in NFL history happened in 1982. What was the effect on the Eagles?
3. 1987 brought a second strike that was countered by replacement players. What was the effect on the Eagles?
4. As Leonard Tose drank and gambled his money away, what city did he negotiate with to move the Eagles?
5. Who was offered the head coaching job before Buddy Ryan?
6. Who scored on the longest TD pass in Eagles history?
7. Sixteen years before Tommy Hutton flubbed his hold for a Chris Boniol 22-yard potential game-winning field goal against the Cowboys in 1997, who did the same thing against the Redskins?
8. Who was the Eagles' first official 300-pound player?
9. The Eagles had more players (six) under 5'9" in the 1980s than in any other decade. How many can you name?
10. Just as in the previous decade, the Eagle who played in the most games in the 1980s was an unsung guard. Who was he?

 OVERTIME: *Uniform Number Question:* While Tommy Thompson was in World War II, the Eagles' starting quarterback wore 7. Who was this former Redskin?

TRIVIA QUIZ 8

THE 1990s

Philadelphia experienced its second consecutive winning decade in the 1990s, going 80-79-1 and again making the playoffs four times. Out was Buddy Ryan and in was Rich Kotite, followed by Ray Rhodes and finally Andy Reid. The team began the 1990s as a rough, tough band of under-achievers who never had a coach who would help them attain their potential and ended the decade with a new coach and new hope once again.

1. What respected veteran defensive coordinator took control of Buddy Ryan's defense in 1991?
2. What defensive coordinator interviewed to replace Ryan?
3. Who brought the West Coast Offense to Philadelphia?
4. How did Barry Switzer achieve moronic immortality in Philadelphia?
5. What former Eagle beat writer won greater acclaim as the author of *Black Hawk Down*?
6. Rank the top Eagle sackers of the 1990s: William Fuller, Andy Harmon, Seth Joyner, Mike Mamula, Clyde Simmons, Reggie White and Willie Thomas.
7. Who was the first NFL player to have 90-yard scoring plays via a run, a reception and a return in one season?
8. "For who? For what?" By whom? About what?
9. What future Eagle finished the "Body Bag Game" as the Redskin quarterback?
10. What was special about Philadelphia's offense in 1998?

OVERTIME: *Uniform Number Question:* The lightest player in Eagle history wore 8. Who was this mighty mite?

TRIVIA QUIZ 9

THE 2000s

THE NEW GLORY DAYS have sprouted under the leadership of Andy Reid. The Eagles made the playoffs in the first five years of the decade and the Super Bowl in 2004. Of course, in 2005, everything came crashing down, partly caused by the well-publicized antics of ego-driven star receiver Terrell Owens. It's up to Reid to right the ship following all the turmoil. Six years into the decade, the Eagles' record is 65-31 in the regular season and 7-5 in the postseason.

1. What coach did Andy Reid pass in 2004 to become the all-time winningest Eagle coach?
2. What thorn in the side of Jeffrey Lurie and Joe Banner began broadcasting in its present format in 1991?
3. In the exciting division-clinching victory over the Giants on December 30, 2001, who knocked Ron Dixon out of bounds at the 6 yard line as time ran out?
4. What Cowboy "horse collared" Terrell Owens in 2004 and finished Donovan McNabb with an interception in 2005?
5. What trick of the 1970s Raiders did the Eagles duplicate in this decade?
6. No player in NFL history had ever recorded an interception, sack, fumble recovery and TD reception in the same game before this Eagle did in 2002. Who is he?
7. Who is officially the heaviest Eagle ever?
8. What did the Eagles give up to obtain Terrell Owens in 2004?
9. How many games was Terrell Owens suspended for in 2005?
10. What Eagle has played in every game from 2000 to 2005?

 OVERTIME: *Uniform Number Question:* 9 was worn by what quarterback from the "Miracle of the Meadowlands"?

TRIVIA QUIZ 10

THE PLAYING FIELD

THE EAGLES HAVE CALLED SEVEN football stadiums home over their long history. How well do you remember these fan havens?

1. The Eagles shared their first home with the Phillies. What was it called?
2. That first home sat 20,000, but their next home field could seat 100,000. What was it known as?
3. Despite the 100,000 capacity, what was the largest crowd the Eagles drew there from 1936 to 1939?
4. In 1940, the Eagles moved back to North Philadelphia to a park with a capacity of 39,000. What was that park called then? What Eagle owner would buy it years later?
5. Due to the declining neighborhood and lack of parking in North Philadelphia, where did the Birds fly to next?
6. How much did attendance per game jump after their move in 1958?
7. In 1971, the Eagles went back to their roots by sharing digs with the Phillies again at Veterans Stadium. What was the cost of this multi-use facility?
8. Who won the first regular season football game at the Vet?
9. What did Eagle fans sing that day to christen the new stadium?
10. Match the strangeness to the venue:
    a. Peepholes into the cheerleaders' dressing room from the visitors' locker room.
    b. Eagle fans throw snowballs at Santa.
    c. A fan runs onto the field to spread his mother's ashes.
    d. Eagle fans throw snowballs at Jimmy Johnson.
    e. Airplanes pass overhead trailing "Joe Must Go" banners.
    f. Eagles cancel a preseason game due to turf problems.

 OVERTIME: *Uniform Number Question:* What quarterback from the 1940s switched to 11 from 10 after being discharged from the military?

SECTION II

GLORY AND RIVALRIES

TRIVIA QUIZ 11

BACK-TO-BACK CHAMPIONSHIPS

THE EAGLES HAVE WON only three championships in their 70+-year history, but two of them came consecutively at the close of the 1940s in the immediate post-World War II era. In fact, half the team had served in the military during the war, including Hall of Fame end Pete Pihos, who served under General Patton, and one-eyed quarterback Tommy Thompson. They were truly battle-hardened and ready for anything. America's "Greatest Generation" was the Eagles' as well.

1. Why was 1947 so frustrating to Greasy Neale?
2. Who cleared the field of snow before the 1948 championship game at Shibe Park?
3. What play set up the only score in the 1948 title game?
4. Why did Greasy Neale want to postpone the 1948 game?
5. Pete Pihos caught a 31-yard TD pass for the first score in the 1949 title match. Who scored the second TD?
6. What cheated the Eagles out of a big pay day in 1949?
7. Why did Bert Bell insist that both the 1948 and 1949 games not be postponed?
8. How many yards did Steve Van Buren run for in 1949 and who broke this record?
9. Who was the Eagles' captain on their title teams?
10. What other team has achieved back-to-back shutouts in winning championships?

 OVERTIME: *Uniform Number Question:* Who was the next quarterback to wear 11 after Norm Van Brocklin?

══ TRIVIA QUIZ 12 ══
1960

SURELY **1960** WAS THE MOST charmed year in Eagle history. A Cinderella team of overachievers went all the way to the title. In terms of talent, the only really special area for the 1960 Eagles was its passing game with Hall of Fame quarterback Norm Van Brocklin throwing to Hall of Fame flanker Tommy McDonald and All-Pro ends Pete Retzlaff and Bobby Walston. No one predicted a championship for this Eagle team but through experienced and passionate leadership and dedicated effort, they pulled it off.

1. Who did the Eagle fans boo in the 1960 opening game loss and why?
2. How did the Eagles beat a terrible Cowboy team in week two?
3. What was their longest winning streak during the season?
4. How many of those wins were the result of fourth-quarter comebacks?
5. What was the team rushing average and who was the team rushing leader?
6. Where did the defense rank in points allowed?
7. In the championship against the Packers, which team had more yards, more first downs, and completed a higher percentage of passes?
8. What insight from assistant coach Charlie Gauer helped win the game?
9. Who scored the winning touchdown?
10. What player played the game despite having to deal with a terrible family tragedy the week before?

 OVERTIME: *Uniform Number Question:* From whom did Randall Cunningham take 12 in 1985? He is one of three Eagle quarterbacks from an Ivy League school.

1980 SEASON: SUPER BOWL XV

TWENTY YEARS AFTER THE 1960 championship, the Eagles returned to the title game, although it was now a much bigger "ultimate game" experience. Once again, the Eagles were a team of overachievers led by a fiery quarterback obtained from the Rams and a vocal, hard-hitting veteran linebacker. As good as he was, though, Ron Jaworski was not Van Brocklin and the battered Bill Bergey was not Bednarik. The Birds lost 27-10.

1. When the Eagles and Raiders met in the 1980 regular season, what was the result?

2. Aside from Harold Carmichael, what was the condition of the receiving corps?

3. When did Jaworski throw his first interception to linebacker Rod Martin?

4. As Jim Plunkett scrambled in the first quarter, he lofted a pass just over whose fingertips to running back Kenny King? What happened next?

5. Near the end of the first half losing 14-3, the Eagles got Tony Franklin in position for a 28-yard field goal. What happened?

6. With the score 21-3 in the third quarter, the Eagles drove into Raiders territory. Jaws tried another pass to John Spagnola and what happened?

7. Finally, in the fourth quarter, the Eagles completed a successful 88-yard drive with a touchdown scored by whom?

8. Rod Martin had twice intercepted passes intended for John Spagnola. For his third pick, who was the intended receiver?

9. The Eagles ran for 254 yards in the NFC Championship against Dallas. How many yards did they gain on the ground in the Super Bowl?

10. Who threw for more yards in the game, Jaworski or Plunkett? Who threw more TD passes?

 OVERTIME: *Uniform Number Question:* What receiver who wore 13 for the Eagles later died on the field during a game?

2004 SEASON: SUPER BOWL XXXIX

IT *ONLY* **TOOK ANOTHER 24 YEARS** to get back to the Super Bowl. In 2004, the Eagles had endured three straight losses in conference championship games, the last two at home, but were a confident, dominating bunch all year. Besides a great defense, the team had finally gotten a number one receiver in Terrell Owens. In fact, they had gotten the best number one receiver in the league and seemed almost unbeatable before he went down with a broken bone in his leg in the 14th game of the year. The Eagles swept through the playoffs without him, but were happy to have him return for the Super Bowl.

1. What's the most obvious common thread between Ron Jaworski and Donovan McNabb's Super Bowl experiences?
2. What mouthy Eagle receiver scored twice against Minnesota in the divisional playoff?
3. What quiet Eagle receiver caught two touchdowns against Atlanta in the conference championship? Why were they bittersweet?
4. Who caught the most passes in the Super Bowl?
5. Who caught TD passes from McNabb that day?
6. Down by 10 with 5:40 to play, how long did it take for the Eagles to score?
7. Armed with two timeouts, the Eagles elected to try an onside kick. Who recovered it?
8. After stopping the Patriots' last drive, where did the Eagles get the ball?
9. How many seconds ran off the clock when McNabb threw the ball back to Brian Westbrook in the middle of the field at the 5 yard line?
10. Whose interception ended the game?

 OVERTIME: *Uniform Number Question:* 14 was worn by an Eagle who kicked for Vermeil in the Super Bowl. Who was he?

TRIVIA QUIZ 15

THE EAGLES IN THE PLAYOFFS

THE EAGLES HAVE BEEN to the postseason 19 times in their history. In six of those seasons, they made it to the championship game, winning three titles. Their overall playoff record is 16-16 through the 2005 season. A Philly fan might look at that as a 3-16 playoff record since championships are the real "gold standard" in Philadelphia. Nonetheless, Eagle playoff games have been flush with exciting and excruciating plays and players.

1. The first time the Eagles made the postseason since the 1960 championship was in 1978 when punter Mike Michel missed an extra point and a last-minute chip-shot field goal on a rainy, muddy day to cause the Eagles to lose 14-13. Why was the punter being used as the placekicker? When did that start?

2. Even though the Eagles ultimately lost the Super Bowl, the 1980 playoffs are remembered fondly because the Eagles beat Dallas. The Birds asserted control early with Wilbert Montgomery's 42-yard cutback run for a touchdown in the first quarter. What was the score at halftime?

3. In 1981 against the Giants, whose fumbles put the Eagles behind early?

4. In the Fog Bowl in 1988, Randall Cunningham threw first-quarter touchdown passes to Cris Carter and Mike Quick, but neither counted. Why?

5. What two Eagle defensive players scored in the lone playoff victory achieved by the Eagle team built by Buddy Ryan?

6. In the Eagles' 58-37 stomping of Detroit in 1995, how many turnovers did the Eagle defense produce and how many points came off of them?

7. Ty Detmer did something dispiriting twice in 1996 against the 49ers. What was it?

8. The 2000, 2001 and 2002 playoffs each featured a key interception clinching the opponent's victory over the Eagles. What three cornerbacks nabbed those three picks?

9. Down 17-14 with 1:12 to play against the Packers in 2003, the Eagles faced a fourth and 26 from their own 26. Did Freddie Mitchell's conversion lead to the winning score?

10. In the 2003 Conference Championship against Carolina, who

caught more passes from Donovan McNabb: James Thrash, Todd Pinkston or Ricky Manning, Jr.?

OVERTIME: *Uniform Number Question:* 15 was worn by the first Eagle to act in Hollywood. Who was this cinematic giant?

—— TRIVIA QUIZ 16 ——

RIVALS: THE COWBOYS

NO TEAM QUITE BRINGS OUT THE HATRED of Eagle fans like the Cowboys. Much of it comes from the perceived imperious, arrogant attitude of Cowboy players and coaches, dating back to the late 1960s. Although the main rival for Dallas has been Washington, Philadelphia has used Dallas as a discouraging measuring stick for decades. Even with Andy Reid having beaten the Cowboys 10 of 14 times in his first seven years, Dallas still holds the advantage at 39-51 through 2005. As the Philly chant goes, "Dallas Sucks."

1. What incident provoked the rivalry with Dallas in 1967?
2. What rookie cornerback gave up three long touchdown passes against the Cowboys in 1970?
3. How did Harold Carmichael's streak of 127 consecutive games with a reception end?
4. After Buddy Ryan had Randall Cunningham throw long after a fake kneel-down at the end of a 1987 win over Dallas, who scored the in-your-face touchdown? Why was Ryan upset?
5. The Eagles sacked Troy Aikman 11 times in one game in 1991. Who led the Eagles in sacks that day?
6. Who put the lick on Michael Irvin that ended his career?
7. How many times did the Eagles beat the Cowboys between 1967 and 1978?
8. How long was Tony Franklin's field goal before the half in the Eagles' 31-21 *Monday Night Football* win at Dallas in 1979?

9. Andy Reid has hung 40 points on Dallas four times. How many times had the Eagles scored 40 points against the Cowboys before Reid arrived in 1999?

10. The longest interception return in team history clinched a win over the Cowboys in 1996. Who intercepted the ball and who scored?

 OVERTIME: *Uniform Number Question:* 16 was worn by what Eagle whose father was a U.S. congressman after his professional football career?

TRIVIA QUIZ
RIVALS: THE GIANTS

The Eagles' oldest rivals are the New York Giants whom they played in their very first game in 1933. Besides the normal Philadelphia distaste for all things New York, the Eagles and Giants have been divisional rivals for over 70 years and both normally live up to their reputations as hard-hitting teams with tough defenses. The two have played a lot of rough games over the course of the series that stands at 67-77-2 in New York's favor through 2005.

1. The Eagles lost their first game ever in October 1933 by a score of 56-0 to the Giants. What was the score of the rematch two months later?

2. Who was the first Eagle coach to achieve a winning record against the Giants?

3. Norm Willey claims to have sacked the Giant quarterbacks 17 times on October 26, 1952. Who were the bruised New York signal callers that day?

4. Tommy McDonald, who regularly tormented the Giants, set an all-time Eagles receiving record against them in 1961. What was this record?

5. The first Eagle to throw for 400 yards in a game did so against the Giants. Who and when?

6. When Chuck Bednarik buried Frank Gifford in 1960, who threw the

pass and who recovered the fumble?

7. To whom was Joe Pisarcik attempting to hand off when the "Miracle of the Meadowlands" occurred?

8. How did Eagle kicker Luis Zendejas win a game by having a field goal blocked in overtime in 1988?

9. What Giants assistant coach did the Eagles deem worthy of a draft pick and how high was the draft pick?

10. Three of the four longest punt returns in team history occurred against the Giants, and three of the five longest pass plays. What eight Eagles returned those punts, threw those passes and caught those touchdowns?

 OVERTIME: *Uniform Number Question:* 17 was first worn by what All-Pro end from Texas who was the first Eagle to record a 100-yard receiving game?

═══ TRIVIA QUIZ ═══

RIVALS: THE REDSKINS

THE REDSKINS STARTED PLAYING the season before the Eagles did, and the two have been divisional rivals for over 70 years. These teams have played many electrifying games throughout the series, with game after game coming down to the wire. The two also have made a fair amount of significant player trades over the years. Washington led the series 59-73-6 through 2005.

1. The biggest deficit the Eagles have ever overcome in a game is 24 points, and they have done that twice. The first time was against Washington. Who was the quarterback that led the Eagle comeback?

2. The Eagles ended a game in 1959 with a memorable goal-line stand. What Redskin runner did the Eagles stonewall three times from the one yard line?

3. Sonny Jurgensen hit Tommy McDonald on a 41-yard crossing pattern for the winning touchdown with 12 seconds left in 1961. What

Redskin corner that would later join the Eagles did they victimize?

4. Who was the first coach of both the Redskins and Eagles?
5. What was the result the first time these two teams met and what year was that?
6. The last game of 1940 was the last game of Davey O'Brien's career. What NFL game records did he set against the Redskins that day?
7. In 1947, the Eagles and Redskins set NFL game records for points, touchdowns and touchdown passes. What rookie was the star of the game?
8. Adrian Burk threw seven touchdown passes against the Redskins in a game in October 1954. How many did he throw in the rematch in November? How had the Eagles acquired Burk?
9. Joe Kuharich coached the Redskins and Eagles for five years each. Where did he do better?
10. What Eagle/Redskin/Eagle clinched the Birds' first-ever win at Lincoln Financial Field with a touchdown?

 OVERTIME: *Uniform Number Question:* Three Eagle kickers later kicked for Dallas (Dick Bielski, Mike Clark and Luis Zendejas) while three Cowboy kickers later kicked for Philadelphia: Sam Baker, Roger Ruzek and what dud who wore 18?

SECTION III

PLAYERS AND POSITIONS

TRIVIA QUIZ 19

CHUCK BEDNARIK

CHUCK BEDNARIK IS MR. EAGLE, the player who most personifies the team, its fans and its city. There was never any doubt about the toughness of this son of Slovak immigrants from Bethlehem, Pa. who served in World War II as a B-24 waist gunner and went to the University of Pennsylvania on the GI Bill. He was a two-way star at Penn and a perennial All-Pro who was elected to the Pro Football Hall of Fame in his first year of eligibility. He is such a local legend that some common knowledge about him has gotten exaggerated. Let's try some true/false questions about Concrete Charlie.

1. At Penn, Bednarik intercepted 13 passes in his junior and senior years and drew an unsportsmanlike conduct penalty in one game for throwing a ball into the stands.

2. Chuck was a two-time All-American as a two-way center/linebacker in college. He was the first lineman to win the Maxwell Award as the best college player.

3. After being selected as the very first pick in the NFL draft, Chuck was such a big star that he started immediately for the 1949 defending champion Eagles.

4. Bednarik played middle linebacker for most of his career.

5. Bednarik was widely regarded as the top center in the league.

6. Chuck retired in 1959.

7. Bednarik's pulverizing hit on Frank Gifford in the 1960 Giants game was the only fumble Chuck caused that day.

8. Chuck played both ways all year in 1960.

9. Bednarik made the final tackle of the NFL title game singlehandedly at the goal line and held Packer fullback Jim Taylor down for several seconds till the game ended.

10. Chuck's recent feud with the Eagles stems from extra warehouse copies of his autobiography from 1976.

 OVERTIME: *Uniform Number Question:* The Eagles have employed two kickers without toes. The second wore 19. Who were these two kickers?

STEVE VAN BUREN

BUCKO KILROY REFERRED TO STEVE VAN BUREN as the Eagles' "paycheck," because the success of the team so depended on him. In fact, what most led to the swift decline of the Eagles in 1950 and 1951 were the injuries suffered by Van Buren in those years. Without Steve, the offense was decapitated. As a runner, Van Buren was a very modern combination of speed and power, and Philadelphia's run-oriented offense stalled quickly without him.

1. Where was Van Buren born?

2. Why did Steve fail to make his high school team as a junior and what did he do about it?

3. At LSU, Steve was a blocking back until his senior year for what future baseball star?

4. In the 1944 Orange Bowl, Steve did something he would duplicate in the 1949 NFL title game. What was it?

5. Although the Eagles selected Steve in the first round of the NFL draft, why did Uncle Sam pass him over in the military draft during World War II?

6. How many interceptions did Van Buren grab as a rookie in 1944?

7. Only Timmy Brown tops Steve in an obscure category in the Eagle record book. What is it?

8. In his second season, Steve set a new NFL record for TDs. How many times did he score in 1945?

9. In 1947, Steve became the second NFL back ever to do something. What was it?

10. To what legendary player did both Greasy Neale and his assistant John Kellison compare Van Buren? What legendary NFL player broke Steve's all-time rushing record?

 OVERTIME: *Uniform Number Question:* 20 was worn by which college great that the Eagles ended up with instead of O.J. Simpson?

NORM VAN BROCKLIN

NORM VAN BROCKLIN HAD A SHORT TENURE in Philadelphia, but many consider him the greatest Eagle quarterback of all because of how he managed to drive a mediocre team to a most improbable championship. He was brash, testy and impatient on the field, but he knew how to win. He and Sonny Jurgensen are the two Eagle quarterbacks in the Hall of Fame.

1. Van Brocklin had starred for the Rams for several seasons, but his personality did not mesh well with Ram coach Sid Gilman, so he welcomed a trade. Who was the Ram GM who made the trade with Philadelphia?

2. The one qualifier Van Brocklin put on his trade request was that he not be sent to Pittsburgh or Philadelphia. Bert Bell got involved in the negotiations and offered what sweetener to entice Van Brocklin to accept the deal?

3. Van Brocklin was also a teacher. What halfback and fullback was he instrumental in converting to receivers?

4. What other duty did Van Brocklin perform on the field for the Eagles?

5. During the 1960 season, Van Brocklin regularly gathered most of the team at what bar in West Philadelphia for socializing?

6. Before Montana and Elway, there was Van Brocklin to specialize in the fourth-quarter comeback. The most important one was against the Browns in Cleveland. Who scored the winning points?

7. Van Brocklin hit two deep balls against the Packers in the title game. One was the 35-yard touchdown to Tommy McDonald. Who caught the other one?

8. Who else retired immediately after the 1960 championship?

9. Although the Eagles offered him another playing contract, where did Van Brocklin go?

10. In 13 years as an NFL head coach, how many winning seasons did Van Brocklin produce?

 OVERTIME: *Uniform Number Question:* What undrafted free agent was heartbroken when he was cut by Vince Lombardi in Green Bay, but went on to play seven hearty years in Philadelphia?

TRIVIA QUIZ 22

TOMMY McDONALD

TOMMY McDONALD MAY HAVE BEEN THE BIGGEST character on a team of characters. He was known for his spontaneous, exuberant approach to life and football. He was fast, shifty and had great hands and reflexes. Although his small size (5'9") kept the team from recognizing how to utilize him at first, he was surprisingly strong, undeniably tough and had a special nose for the end zone. After a long wait, McDonald finally was elected to the Hall of Fame in 1998.

1. How many games did Tommy McDonald lose in his college career?
2. What major awards did McDonald win in college?
3. Who was Tommy mistaken for when he came to Philadelphia to negotiate his contract?
4. When did McDonald get his first chance to play receiver and how did he do?
5. What common piece of football equipment did McDonald avoid?
6. Rank these Eagle receivers by their touchdown percentage: Jack Ferrante, Tommy McDonald, Harold Carmichael, Mike Quick and Cris Carter.
7. Terrell Owens broke McDonald's team record for touchdown catches in a season in 2004. What year did Tommy set the record?
8. How many times did McDonald lead the league in touchdown catches?
9. When Tommy chest-bumped his fellow inductees at his Hall of Fame induction, it was reminiscent of what practice of his as a player?
10. At the Hall of Fame induction ceremony in 1998, what song did McDonald play on his boombox and dance to on stage?

 OVERTIME: *Uniform Number Question:* This undersized Tongan who wore 22 in Philadelphia is remembered for his boxing match with a goal post. Who was he?

HAROLD CARMICHAEL
AND WILBERT MONTGOMERY

HAROLD CARMICHAEL WAS a 6'8" receiver out of a small school who was first tried at tight end by the Eagles and found wanting before switching to wide receiver and becoming a star and the team's all-time leading receiver. Wilbert Montgomery was 10 inches shorter than Carmichael and had a stockier body type, but was a fast, powerful and elusive runner and receiver. Together, they represented the offense of Dick Vermeil's resurgent Eagles of the late 1970s.

1. What Eagle assistant coach advocated the move of Carmichael to wide receiver in 1973?
2. How did Harold show that he had arrived in his third season?
3. In 1979, Harold broke what record of New Orleans Saint Dan Abramowicz?
4. How tall was the trophy the Eagles presented to him and what happened to it?
5. Whom did Carmichael pass to become the all-time leading Eagles receiver?
6. How many brothers of Wilbert Montgomery played in the NFL?
7. How many touchdowns did Wilbert score as a college freshman? How many for his college career?
8. How did the Eagles acquire the draft pick they used to select Wilbert in 1977?
9. Wilbert first gained over 1,000 yards in 1978. Who was the last Eagle before him to reach this seasonal milestone?
10. How many times did he lead the Eagles in rushing? How many times did he exceed 1,000 yards?

OVERTIME: *Uniform Number Question:* This number one draft pick from 1967 averaged less than two yards per carry over four seasons as an Eagle. Who represented 23 in this sad way?

BILL BERGEY

BILL BERGEY WAS THE GREATEST middle linebacker the Eagles have ever had. He was a vocal, enthusiastic leader on the field and one of the hardest hitters the Eagle fans have ever seen. Before his knee injury, Bergey was fast enough to drop into pass coverage and quick enough to fill the running lanes. Above all, Bergey was so intense on the field that the fans could feel it in the stands, and he was a fan favorite who inspired "Bergey's Brawlers" signs to pop up at the Vet in the 1970s.

1. Bergey attended Arkansas State and shared a nickname with a certain Arkansas governor who became President of the U.S. What were these two Bills called?

2. Where did Bergey begin his career?

3. What rival league brought him to Philadelphia?

4. What did the Eagles give up to get Bill?

5. Early on, the Eagle linebacking corps was known as the Bergey Bunch and had a Butch Cassidy-style photo taken in 1975. Who were the members of the Bergey Bunch?

6. How many times did Bill lead the Eagles in tackles?

7. How many times was he All-Pro?

8. What was his last game as an Eagle?

9. When did he retire?

10. In addition to doing the Eagle pregame radio show, the Bergey name has stayed in the public because his sons play what sport locally?

OVERTIME: *Uniform Number Question:* The first black NFL quarterback employed by the Eagles played defensive back for them and wore 24 briefly. Who was he?

TRIVIA QUIZ 25

RON JAWORSKI

RON JAWORSKI WAS KNOWN AS JAWS for his talkative nature, but was a tough guy who didn't complain despite being sacked nearly 400 times in his 15-year career. Despite being a blue-collar-type guy, Jaworski still was heavily booed at times in his 10 years in Philadelphia. To his credit, he was able to shake it off and become a favorite of local fans long after his playing days ended. As a player, he was a hard-working overachiever who took the Eagles to a Super Bowl. In retirement, Jaws settled in the Philadelphia area and has been successful in the business world while maintaining a visible public image on ESPN as an impressively incisive and lively football commentator known for his detailed film study.

1. Jaworski was drafted by what team in which round in 1973?
2. Who did the Eagles give up to obtain him?
3. How many times was he sacked as an Eagle?
4. How many concussions did he suffer in his career?
5. Brett Favre holds the record for consecutive starts by an NFL quarterback and broke the record held by Jaworski. How many games did Jaws start consecutively?
6. What award did Jaworski win in 1980?
7. How many times did he top 20 touchdown passes? Or 20 interceptions?
8. How many categories did Jaws lead the league in over his career?
9. What three quarterbacks did Jaws back up in his last three years in the league?
10. He was once a candidate for the Eagles GM, but now holds that position for what team?

 OVERTIME: *Uniform Number Question:* was the first number worn by an Eagle best known for wearing 44. Who is this former Eagle GM?

REGGIE WHITE

WITH THE POSSIBLE EXCEPTION of Chuck Bednarik, Reggie White is the only Eagle who would receive serious consideration as the greatest to ever play his position. White was a unique combination of speed and power rarely found in a man his size. He was equally adept at stopping the run and rushing the passer and was shuffled along the defensive line to fit the needs of the team. On almost every play, he was double- or triple-teamed and thus made the entire defense around him better. Although a spiritual man, he had a strong sense of humor and was a natural leader of every team on which he played. His death at 43 came as a shock to all football fans.

1. In what draft did the Eagles acquire his rights?
2. How many sacks did he record in 1985?
3. What number did he wear in his first game?
4. What was the lowest sack total he achieved in any season as an Eagle?
5. What were his two nicknames?
6. What was most remarkable about his Eagle seasonal sack record?
7. How many Pro Bowls was he named to consecutively?
8. How many times did he retire?
9. What is his lasting effect on the NFL Players' Union?
10. The Eagles retired his number at halftime of what game?

OVERTIME: *Uniform Number Question:* What defensive back who wore 26 is best remembered for returning two missed field goals for touchdowns?

TRIVIA QUIZ 27

RANDALL CUNNINGHAM

RANDALL CUNNINGHAM WAS CALLED "Starship 12" by former Eagle player and broadcaster Stan Walters for his flaky behavior, but *Sports Illustrated* anointed him the "Ultimate Weapon" when he was at his peak. No other Eagle has evoked such a wide discrepancy among the opinions of fans. To some he was the greatest quarterback in Eagle history who would have led the team to multiple championships if he only had received better coaching. To others, Cunningham was a tremendous athlete who could have been great if he had been more disciplined and applied himself to his craft, instead of simply craving celebrity.

1. On what team did his older brother play?

2. When Randall hurdled the Giants' Carl Banks to throw a touchdown pass, to whom did he throw the ball?

3. What future Hall of Famer did Randall elude to throw a 95-yard TD to Fred Barnett?

4. Two of the three longest punts in Eagle history were by Cunningham. How far did they travel?

5. How many yards did he throw for in the Fog Bowl? How many touchdowns?

6. How many consecutive seasons did Randall lead the Eagles in rushing?

7. When Randall retired from the Eagles in 1995, what did he go into?

8. Which training camp slogan was the title of his autobiography: "Any questions, call my agent," "Let me be me," or "I'm still scrambling"?

9. One year, he got permission from Buddy Ryan to leave an exhibition game early to attend whose birthday party?

10. How many times did he win the Bert Bell Trophy as NFL MVP?

 OVERTIME: *Uniform Number Question:* 27 was worn by a running back who ran the 100 in 9.6 and played for Navy and Arkansas. The latter retired his number. Who was he?

DONOVAN McNABB

DONOVAN McNABB HAS BEEN the subject of a storm of controversy since the moment he was drafted when a group of extreme Eagle fans bused to the draft by WIP sportstalk radio roundly booed the selection. While McNabb did not outwardly react to this embarrassing beginning, he has let on in the ensuing years that he will never forget his introduction to Philadelphia. Until 2005, McNabb's career showed a steady upward progression toward superstardom. After the meltdown of 2005, though, the pressure is on McNabb again to perform.

1. What other sport did Donovan McNabb play in college?
2. Five quarterbacks were picked in the first round of the 1999 NFL draft. Which quarterbacks were picked ahead of McNabb?
3. Who was the last quarterback picked in the first round by the Eagles?
4. Everyone remembers Rush Limbaugh's comments about the media bending over backwards to support McNabb because they wanted a black quarterback to succeed. However, who was the first person to bring up racial issues around McNabb?
5. How many times has McNabb led the team in rushing?
6. McNabb led the Eagles to the playoffs for five straight years, 2000 to 2004. What Eagle quarterback did he surpass?
7. What was special about Donovan's four touchdown passes against the Cardinals in 2002?
8. In how many categories has McNabb led the NFL?
9. Rank these Eagle quarterbacks by their highest passing yardage total in a championship game: Tommy Thompson, Norm Van Brocklin, Ron Jaworski and Donovan McNabb.
10. In the midst of Terrell Owens' antics to get a new contract in 2005, he gave an interview in which he agreed that the Eagles would be better with Brett Favre as quarterback. When McNabb finally responded two months later, what was the oddest thing about his response?

OVERTIME: *Uniform Number Question:* What star safety who wore 28 for the Eagles and led the NFL in interceptions was related to a five-star general prominent in World War II?

EAGLE QUARTERBACKS

WHILE PHILLY FANS HAVE ENJOYED the exploits of such star quarterbacks as Tommy Thompson, Norm Van Brocklin, Sonny Jurgensen, Ron Jaworski, Randall Cunningham and Donovan McNabb over the years, we also have witnessed quarterback depravity and horror that incites the booing for which we are so famous. Eagle quarterbacks have run the gamut in skills and performance.

1. Rank these four quarterbacks by their lowest seasonal quarterback rating: Tommy Thompson, Adrian Burk, Bobby Thomason and Bobby Hoying.

2. Who was the first black quarterback to take a snap for the Eagles?

3. Which of these passers won the Heisman Trophy: Davey O'Brien, Sonny Jurgensen, John Huarte, John Reaves, Ty Detmer or Koy Detmer?

4. Which of these quarterbacks did not win the Davey O'Brien Award for best college quarterback: Jim McMahon, Don McPherson, Ty Detmer or Donovan McNabb?

5. Which of these quarterbacks did not win the Johnny Unitas Award for best college quarterback: Don McPherson, Rodney Peete, Casey Weldon or Donovan McNabb?

6. For what backup quarterback who had thrown one pass in an NFL game did the Eagles give up two second-round picks and a third rounder in 1971?

7. Which of these quarterbacks did not cost the Eagles a first-round draft pick: Bobby Thomason, Norm Van Brocklin, King Hill, Roman Gabriel, Mike Boryla or Matt Cavanaugh?

8. Which of these quarterbacks did not come right from the Rams to the Eagles: Bobby Thomason, Norm Van Brocklin, Roman Gabriel, Ron Jaworski or Jeff Kemp?

9. Which of these quarterbacks never was named to the Pro Bowl: Adrian Burk, Bobby Thomason, Norm Snead, Mike Boryla or Rodney Peete?

10. Who was the first Eagle to throw 25 touchdown passes?

OVERTIME: *Uniform Number Question:* 29 was worn by a 5'7" cornerback who was more of a hot dog than a big dog. Who was he?

EAGLE RUNNING BACKS

FOR A BLUE-COLLAR TOWN that favors smashmouth football, Philadelphia's Eagles have usually struggled to develop a presentable running game. Hall of Famer Steve Van Buren is the only Eagle ever to lead the NFL in rushing, and there have been precious few 1,000-yard rushers in Eagle history. From Timmy Brown through Wilbert Montgomery and Brian Westbrook, though, the Birds do have a tradition for smallish runners who are just as good catching passes out of the backfield as running the ball from scrimmage.

1. Who was the first Eagle to lead the team in rushing and how many times did he do it?

2. These Eagle runners have all led the team in rushing at least three times: Swede Hanson, Billy Ray Barnes, Tom Woodeshick, Timmy Brown, Tom Sullivan, Randall Cunningham and Brian Westbrook. What else do they have in common?

3. What 1,000-yard rusher was cut the next season?

4. What's the lowest team-leading rushing total since 1946?

5. What's the lowest yards-per-carry average by a runner who led the Eagles in rushing after 1946?

6. Who led the league in rushing average in 1949?

7. Who set an NFL record with 2,306 total yards in 1962 and topped it the following season with 2,428 total yards?

8. What running back caught the most passes as an Eagle?

9. Who was the first running back to rush for over 1,000 yards for three different teams?

10. What three-time Eagle offensive MVP won a Super Bowl ring across the state in Pittsburgh?

OVERTIME: *Uniform Number Question:* 30 was worn by a talented kick returner acquired for Timmy Brown. Who was he?

EAGLE RECEIVERS

FOR ALL THE TROUBLE THE EAGLES have had in finding quality receivers during the Andy Reid era, the franchise has had a number of star receivers throughout its history. Since the end of World War II, the Eagles had a clear number one receiver virtually every year into the Buddy Ryan era. After that, the quality at wide receiver has been thin, especially since the West Coast Offense was introduced to Philadelphia a decade ago. That's ironic since the West Coast Offense so emphasizes passing—especially Andy Reid's version of the scheme.

1. Who was the first Eagle to lead the NFL in a receiving category and to catch 100 passes for his career?

2. What Hall of Famer caught half of 102 passes with the Bears and half with the Eagles?

3. What Eagle Hall of Famer led the NFL in receptions for three straight seasons?

4. What Eagle receiver was once the fastest man in the world?

5. This receiver played for five teams. As an Eagle he led the NFL twice in yards and once in receptions. Who was he?

6. What three Eagle tight ends won the Rookie of the Year award?

7. Who is the only Eagle to catch at least 80 balls two times?

8. In his second season, what Eagle caught 69 passes for 13 touchdowns and a 20 yards-per-catch average?

9. After finishing second in the NFL in catches in his second season, what Eagle receiver jumped to the Canadian Football League?

10. What Eagle tight end's career in Philadelphia lasted six plays of an exhibition game?

OVERTIME: *Uniform Number Question:* 31 was worn by what 1930s player who became famous as a Chicago columnist and TV talk show host?

EAGLE OFFENSIVE LINEMEN

THE QUALITY OF THE EAGLES' OFFENSIVE line has varied widely over the years. Greasy Neale built a terrific line that was essential for his ground-oriented attack. The Eagles' line faded a bit in the 1950s, but was good again under Joe Kuharich who had a respected line coach in Dick Stanfel. Dick Vermeil had a solid line and Andy Reid has done well in this regard as well. By contrast, the lines under Buddy Ryan were never good and played a large role in the ultimate failure of those clubs.

1. Who was the first Eagle lineman named to an All-Pro team?

2. What Eagle center was descended from the Navy admiral who said, "Damn the torpedoes; full speed ahead"?

3. When did the Eagles feature two starting guards who were born in Italy? Who were they?

4. For 35 of the 42 years from 1943 to 1984, 76 was worn by an All-Pro at tackle. Who were these four linemen?

5. This guard started for the last Lions team to win a title and the last Eagles team to win a title.

6. What made tackle Lane Howell notorious in Philadelphia?

7. Between 1941 and 1943, the Eagles' line featured what three teammates from the University of Tennessee?

8. What All-Pro tackle had his number retired both by the Eagles and by the University of Michigan?

9. The oldest Eagle rookie at 35 doubled as the team's trainer in 1946. Who was he?

10. What Eagle guard appeared in several prominent TV westerns and over 50 films, including four with Clint Eastwood?

 OVERTIME: *Uniform Number Question:* 32 was worn by an Eagle runner who was an early proponent of religious celebration on the football field. Who was he?

TRIVIA QUIZ 33

EAGLE DEFENDERS

THE BEST EAGLE TEAMS THROUGHOUT their history have featured tough defenses. Nothing gets a Philly crowd going like a huge defensive stand or a booming, knockout blow delivered by the defense. Greasy Neale's "Eagle Defense" in the 1940s, the bully boys of the 1950s, Marion Campbell's brawlers of the late seventies, Buddy Ryan's bounty hunters and Jim Johnson's blitzers have been the fan favorites and the backbone of winners.

1. Who is tied with Bill Bradley for the all-time team record of 34 interceptions as an Eagle?
2. Who held the team records for interceptions before Bill Bradley passed him?
3. What 1986 eighth-round draft pick cut at the end of training camp and re-signed two weeks later became a starter by midseason, replacing a 1986 second-round pick?
4. Who was the last lineman in the NFL and AFL to not wear a face mask?
5. What Eagles ninth-round pick only made it to college because a recruiter noticed him shooting pool?
6. Which 11-year Eagle veteran finally won a championship in Philadelphia, but in the USFL?
7. Clyde Simmons played with Reggie White. As a kid in North Carolina, he played Babe Ruth League baseball with another all-time great in another sport. Who was he?
8. What veteran defensive end challenged a coach to a fight and quit the team in 1973?
9. Which Eagle defensive back partially fulfilled his military service requirement by assisting Buck Shaw in coaching the very first Air Force Academy football team before playing under Shaw in Philadelphia?
10. Who was the middle linebacker on the 1960 championship team?

 OVERTIME: *Uniform Number Question:* Joe Kuharich coached this Hall of Famer in college and at two stops in the pros, the second of which was Philadelphia. Who was this runner who wore 33?

TRIVIA QUIZ 34

EAGLE KICKERS

KICKERS AND PUNTERS TEND to be the flakiest players on the team. Their tenure on the team is often short-lived depending on their efficiency and the effectiveness of their work on a week-to-week basis. The life of a kicking specialist is pressure-packed. In their one specialized function, they are expected to be perfect from the start and then get better; they can't offset a bad kick by excelling in some other phase of offense or defense, and their mistakes and failures are obvious for all to see.

1. Which Eagle kicker once held the NFL record for consecutive extra-point conversions?
2. In 1961, what Eagle became the NFL's all-time leading scorer? Whom did he pass and who passed him?
3. Who was the last straight-ahead kicker on the Eagles?
4. Who was the first Eagle soccer-style kicker?
5. These two 15-year kickers also each played in Washington. One scored 977 points in the NFL, but never reached 100 in a season; the other won a league MVP award. Who were they?
6. What was the main difference between Tony Franklin and Paul McFadden?
7. The Eagles again had the NFL's eventual all-time leading scorer in 1995-96. Who was he?
8. What Eagles "long-kicking specialist" did not make a field goal in his last four years on the team?
9. Which Eagle kicker sometimes had trouble remembering to go on the field with the field-goal unit?
10. What punter cost the Eagles a draft pick, but not in a trade?

 OVERTIME: *Uniform Number Question:* 34 was worn in 1963 by an Eagle who was traded for a player of a different position who wore 34 in 1964. Who were these players?

SECTION IV

MANAGEMENT

TRIVIA QUIZ 35

OWNERSHIP

THERE HAVE BEEN SEVEN principal owners or ownership groups in the 70+-year history of the Eagles, and they have differed a great deal in terms of effectiveness, creativity, wealth, likeability and class. Some have served the team, the fans and the city well, while others have been little better than stooges and robber barons. The one constant has been the steady rise in the value of the franchise; each owner sold the team for more than he or they paid for it. Some have lost money along the way, but there is always that big capital gain at the end.

1. Which two Eagle owners went bankrupt?
2. Which two Eagle owners attended an Ivy League school?
3. How many investors were in the corporation that bought the Eagles in 1949?
4. What prominent figure from Pittsburgh once owned half of the Philadelphia franchise?
5. What Hall of Fame coach tried to buy the Eagles in the 1960s?
6. What owner competed in the Olympics?
7. What former Eagles owner was outbid to buy the Redskins in 1999?
8. Which owners had a reputation as playboys?
9. Which of these cities have not made a play for the Eagles: Louisville, Phoenix, San Antonio or San Francisco?
10. What Eagle owner set the "gold standard"?

 OVERTIME: *Uniform Number Question:* This rookie runner who wore 35 was the unsung hero of the 1960 championship. Who was this local kid whose bright football future was derailed by injuries?

TRIVIA QUIZ 36

BERT BELL

BERT BELL PLAYED A MAJOR ROLE in the development of the NFL from a second-class league to the most popular sport in the country. Bell came from a well-to-do family in Philadelphia, but he was the black sheep of the family, a loveable rogue who liked to gamble and socialize. He led the group of investors who founded the Eagles and later bought the rest of them out. He became commissioner in 1946 and guided the league through such difficulties as a war with the rival All-America Conference and antitrust exemptions in Congress. He was elected to the Hall of Fame in its first year of existence.

1. What was the highest public office held by Bert Bell's father and brother John?
2. What was Bert's major accomplishment at the University of Pennsylvania?
3. What interrupted Bert's college career?
4. Who hired Bell as an assistant coach at Penn?
5. Where did Bell coach after Penn?
6. How did Bell become coach of the Eagles in 1936? How did he compare to the Eagles' first coach?
7. Why did Bell give up gambling?
8. Why did Bell give up drinking?
9. What was ironic about his death?
10. What was his real first name?

 OVERTIME: *Uniform Number Question:* The only Eagle who ever led the NFL in punting wore 36. Who was this fullback/linebacker?

TRIVIA QUIZ 37

COACHES AND GMs

ONLY SEVEN OF THE 18 EAGLE COACHES who have coached at least 10 games won more games than they lost. Those seven were Andy Reid, Greasy Neale, Rich Kotite, Jim Trimble, Buddy Ryan, Buck Shaw and Dick Vermeil. The Eagles have had coaches who were incompetent, who melted down and who burned out. They've had coaches who've been to the Rose Bowl, the CFL Grey Cup and the Super Bowl. They've had coaches who spoke in sound bites, who spoke in malaprops and who hardly spoke at all. They've had coaches who screamed, who celebrated and who cried—sometimes all on the same day. They've had GMs who were secretive, loyal, invisible and inscrutable. They've had every sort of combination except one that won a Super Bowl.

1. How was the Eagles' first coach connected to Bert Bell and Philadelphia?
2. What coach lasted only two games before he had to step down due to illness?
3. What four Eagle coaches played at Notre Dame? What coaches did they play under in South Bend?
4. What two assistant coaches from the 1960 team later headed the Eagles?
5. What two defensive linemen who were teammates later coached the Eagles?
6. Buck Shaw had two conditions before accepting the Eagles' head coaching job. What were they?
7. What Eagle player became Eagle GM?
8. How many winning seasons did Marion Campbell record in his NFL coaching career?
9. Who served longest as Eagle GM?
10. How many personnel people/scouting directors/GMs did the Eagles go through under Jeff Lurie until Andy Reid assumed full control in 2000?

 OVERTIME: *Uniform Number Question:* This Wilkes Barre native had a cousin who was a major league relief pitcher in the 1950s and 1960s. Who was this Eagle who wore 37 most prominently?

TRIVIA QUIZ 38

KUHARICH, KHAYAT AND KOTITE: THREE STRIKEOUTS

THERE HAVE BEEN WORSE EAGLES coaches than the three whose names began with K, but there was something particularly infuriating about this troika. Joe Kuharich emphasized that he didn't want a team of stars whose value "went up and down like the stock market." So he traded away the stars, but rarely got comparable value and left the team in shambles despite having 11 years left on his 15-year contract. Former player Ed Khayat was a play-ers' coach as an assistant, but once he became the head coach he turned into a martinet who seemed more interested in the players' appearance than winning. Rich Kotite has the third highest winning percentage in team history, but that's because he had the unusual distinction of taking over a winning team. So instead of rebuilding a team that was down, he destroyed a team that was very close to the top, and he did so with the personality and panache of a mortician.

1. Who said, "All but a handful of [the players] quit"?
2. Conversely, who said, "They left nothing in the locker room" on a weekly basis?
3. Who said, "Every coach must view a player with three different eyes"?
4. Who said, "We were three points behind, but that's not the same as being even"?
5. Who started many replies with the phrase, "without question"?
6. Who said, "Good grooming is one of the many facets of discipline"?
7. Who said, "It's quite rare, but not unusual"?
8. Which of these three "koaches" was the first Notre Dame coach to leave South Bend with a losing record?
9. While Rich Kotite managed to achieve a winning record in Philadelphia, he lost his last seven games. What was his record at his next stop?
10. How did Joe Kuharich mangle these clichés: "fine kettle of fish," "horse of a different color" and "now the shoe is on the other foot"?

 OVERTIME: *Uniform Number Question:* 38 was worn by what loose cannon who played eight of his 15 NFL years under Joe Kuharich in Washington and Philadelphia?

TRIVIA QUIZ 39

BUDDY RYAN AND DICK VERMEIL

NUMBERS FIVE AND SEVEN on the list of Eagles winning coaches were Buddy Ryan and Dick Vermeil, but they are likely numbers one and two in the hearts of most Eagle fans. Vermeil wore his heart on his sleeve and demonstrated every day how desperately he needed to win. He was a screamer, but he also clearly loved his players, to a sentimental degree at times. The caustic and quotable Ryan was the opposite of Vermeil in personality and was a mirror image of the tough, blustering persona of the Philly fan. He clearly loved his players, too, and that came at the expense of his relationship with a distant autocratic management. Both took over terrible teams and rebuilt them into winners. Moreover, both took special interest in deflating and defeating the Cowboys.

1. Who did Buddy refer to as the "illegitimate son" of "that guy in France"?

2. Of whom did Buddy say, "I'd trade him for a six pack and it wouldn't even have to be cold"?

3. What first-round draft pick did he call a "medical reject" before the draft?

4. What player did he cut because "All he can do is catch touchdowns"?

5. Match these three lesser lights with Buddy's cutting comments: Michael Haddix, Herman Hunter and Alonzo Johnson.

    A. "We believe in giving everybody a chance. This is America, not Russia."

    B. "He looks like a reject guard from the USFL. He's so fat."

    C. "He wasn't blocking in any of the drills. I assumed when the linebackers started blitzing, he'd leave."

6. Dick Vermeil was the first of what type of assistant coach in the NFL?

7. What passing combination led Vermeil's UCLA team to a 1976 Rose Bowl victory?

8. Whom did he choose with his initial first-round draft pick and in what year?

9. What former Eagle player was with Vermeil for every game in Philadelphia, St. Louis and Kansas City?

10. What ticked off Vermeil on July 4, 1976?

OVERTIME: *Uniform Number Question:* What former Eagle water boy wore 39 when he became the first quarterback to lead the Eagles to victory over the Chicago Bears?

TRIVIA QUIZ 40

GREASY NEALE AND ANDY REID

BEFORE ANDY REID CAME ALONG, Greasy Neale was the top Eagles coach both in terms of wins and winning percentage. Until Reid wins a title, Neale will still be the greatest Eagle coach. Neale took over a horrible situation in 1941, a team with no winning tradition and no players with any established talent. The only player he inherited that would still be with him when the team started winning championships was a one-eyed, unsuccessful tailback named Tommy Thompson whom Neale turned into an excellent T-Formation quarterback. Reid also took over a terrible team, but there was talent on it. He improved that talent and added to it so much that the Eagles in the new millennium have been enjoying their second glory days. All that's lacking is a Super Bowl win or two.

1. As a college coach, Neale took what unlikely school to the Rose Bowl?
2. What was Neale's other sports connection to Philadelphia?
3. When did Neale say, "That wasn't a football game out there. With all of their passing, that was more like a basketball game played on a football field"?
4. How did Neale first devise the Eagles' offensive scheme?
5. Did the Eagles ever run the ball less than 60% during Neale's tenure?
6. Andy Reid reportedly impressed Jeff Lurie and Joe Banner with his detailed explanation of what mundane play?
7. What did the Packers do to try to retain Reid?
8. How many touchdown catches did Terrell Owens need to put Andy in black tights in 2004?
9. What one-time Eagle quarterback was Andy's college teammate?
10. What Philadelphia sportscaster played for Brigham Young when Reid coached there?

OVERTIME: *Uniform Number Question:* What former Marine wore 40 with the Eagles from 1949 to 1951 before becoming football coach at Villanova from 1954 to 1959?

===== Trivia Quiz =====

TRADES

ONE WAY TO TRACK THE SUCCESS of a franchise is to track the quality of its trades. Some of the Eagles' unsuccessful front office regimes owe a good part of their failure to bad trades. Joe Kuharich made over 20 deals in his time and most of them were bad; Pete Retzlaff followed him with bad trade after bad trade and Mike McCormack, who came next, emptied the team's future for a piddling present. Greasy Neale and Vince McNally, in the 1940s and 1950s, made some very good deals, while most other regimes were up and down in their trading, some good some bad.

1. Who else was included in the swap of Sonny Jurgensen for Norm Snead?

2. To what team did Joe Kuharich first offer Jurgensen?

3. What did Snead bring in trade seven years later?

4. What did Kuharich get for Hall of Fame receiver Tommy McDonald?

5. Besides a number one pick, what else did the Eagles give up for Norm Van Brocklin? Who did the number one turn out to be?

6. Mike McCormack traded away so many draft picks that the Eagles did not have a first- or second-round pick from 1974 to 1978. What other Eagle coach/GM liked to trade away his top picks?

7. Maxie Baughan had been named All-Pro every year but one when the Eagles dealt him. What did Philadelphia get?

8. Once Baughan went, his friend Irv Cross demanded a trade. What did the Eagles get for their Pro Bowl cornerback?

9. There was great upheaval when Norman Braman bought the team from Leonard Tose. Eleven veterans held out of training camp because of contract disputes tied to promises made by Tose. Nine of those 11 were dispatched from the team including all-time leading rusher Wilbert Montgomery who brought what in return?

10. What was the significance of the trade of Jon Harris for John Michels in 1999?

 OVERTIME: *Uniform Number Question:* This safety who wore 41 was the team's defensive MVP as a rookie in 1973. Who was he?

────── TRIVIA QUIZ ──────
FREE AGENCY

THERE ARE TWO TYPES OF FREE AGENCY. The first has been around since the start of pro football and refers to undrafted rookies. Every year teams sign players who no one drafted to come to training camp to fight for a position. While you usually don't find stars that way, you can find some very useful players, even starters. On the other hand, free agency for veteran players has only really been around for the past 15 years and is a very visible challenge for the team's front office to sign players who will help the team without wrecking the salary cap structure. In recent years, the Eagles have been successful in both areas, but that was not always the case.

1. What undrafted free agent lasted the longest with the team?
2. What undrafted free agent caught a touchdown pass in the Super Bowl?
3. What undrafted free agent has the second highest interception total in team history?
4. What undrafted free agent went on to coach a Super Bowl winner?
5. What undrafted free agent has been portrayed by Mark Wahlberg in a biopic?
6. What undrafted free agent went from being a construction worker to signing a million-dollar contract with the Eagles in four years?
7. Who was the first significant Eagle to leave Philadelphia as a free agent?
8. After winning his landmark lawsuit, Reggie White went to the Packers and the Eagles signed what former Packer to replace him?

9. What free agents replaced the mass exodus of Buddy's boys, Seth Joyner, Clyde Simmons and Andre Waters in 1994?

10. What free agent wide receivers has Andy Reid signed from 1999 to 2005?

 OVERTIME: *Uniform Number Question:* 42 was the first number worn by what running back/H-back/tight end who later played for Miami, New England and the Jets?

===== TRIVIA QUIZ

THE DRAFT

THE NFL PLAYER DRAFT HAS MORE history with the Eagles than with any other team because it was devised by Bert Bell as a way to improve the weaker teams and was instituted at his behest when he was Philadelphia's owner. For the Eagles, the best at getting players from the draft was Greasy Neale, while the best at finding stars was Buddy Ryan. Surprisingly for someone who liked to trade away draft choices, Mike McCormack used the picks he kept pretty well, and Dick Vermeil drafted well also. On the negative side, Joe Kuharich, Pete Retzlaff and Rich Kotite tended to butcher the draft and the team's future was reflected by it. Andy Reid has done pretty well on the whole, although his rating is pending since he is still active.

1. The draft was Bert Bell's baby, and he had the first pick ever in 1936. Whom did he select and how did it work out?

2. For the first time in 1949, the Eagles drafted a quarterback in the first round. Who was he and what Hall of Fame quarterbacks were also available?

3. What was significant about Johnny Bright, the Eagles' first pick in 1952?

4. When the Eagles selected Leonard Mitchell in the first round in 1981, which Hall of Famers could they have selected instead?

5. When the Eagles selected Michael Haddix in the first round in 1983, which Hall of Famers could they have selected instead?

6. Which of these Eagle first-round picks was not a complete flop on the offensive line: Antone Davis (1991), Leonard Renfro (1993), Lester Holmes (1993) or Bernard Williams (1994)?

7. When the Eagles selected tackle Kevin Allen in the first round in 1985, what perennial All-Pro tackle who did not go to prison could they have selected? What Hall of Famer was also available?

8. When the Eagles moved up to grab workout wonder Mike Mamula at number 10 in 1995, what All-Pros did they pass up?

9. How did the Eagles wind up with Mike Quick?

10. Which Eagle who made All-Pro was drafted in the lowest round? Which had the most players selected ahead of him?

 OVERTIME: *Uniform Number Question:* What running back who missed winning the NFL rushing title by one yard wore 43?

SECTION V

THE OFFBEAT

UNIFORM NUMBERS

UNIFORM NUMBERS TAKE ON a superstitious significance to many players, so much so that players frequently make extravagant deals with one another in order to be able to wear the number they want to wear. Moreover, fans not only identify the players by the numbers they wear, but identify with the players by wearing replica jerseys with those numbers themselves. There has even been a history of the team, *Eagles by the Numbers*, which tells the team's story through their uniform numbers. You may have heard of it.

1. Who wore one number longer than any other Eagle?
2. What number was worn by the oldest Eagle?
3. Aside from 0, what number has been worn by the fewest players?
4. Receivers traditionally wear numbers in the 80s, but five of the top 10 Eagle reception leaders among wide receivers did not wear numbers in the 80s. Who were they and what numbers did they wear?
5. What did the Philadelphia Eagles attempt to do with uniform numbers in 1941?
6. Who was the first Eagle to wear a number in the 90s?
7. What was the last number to have been worn by an Eagle?
8. What Hall of Famers have had their uniform numbers retired by the Eagles?
9. What numbers have the Eagles retired for non-Hall of Famers?
10. What number has not been worn by an Eagle for the longest stretch of time?

 OVERTIME: *Uniform Number Question:* What "Wild Man" wore 44 as a rookie?

NICKNAMES

NICKNAMES ARE ONE OF THE FUN PARTS of the game. They may refer to how a player looks, talks or plays, where he's from, how his name sounds or any number of other reasons his teammates have to honor, tease or abuse him. In the past, sportswriters would get into the act, too, devising silly nicknames for players such as "Weavin' Steven the Moving Van" for Steve Van Buren. The only person who still does that sort of thing is Chris Berman of ESPN, but these can be amusing as well.

1. Herman Bassman, Bob Kelley, Roger Kirkman, Bill Mack, Henry Piro, Herschel Ramsey, Albert Weiner—which ones were not known as Red?

2. Marv Elstrom, Tom Hanson and Wayne Robinson all shared what ethnic nickname?

3. What is the connecting thread among the nicknames of David Alexander, Todd Bell, Hank Fraley, Al Harris and Ed Manske?

4. What animal nicknames were these players given: Eric Allen, Walter Barnes, Frank Emmons, Bobby Freeman, Alan Keen, Joe Lavender, John Lipski, George Rado and Al Wistert? What animal part was John Magee called by?

5. What two Eagles were known as the Big Dog?

6. Greg Garrity, Bill Hewitt, Earle Neale and Andre Waters had what filthy nicknames?

7. What were the geographic nicknames of Fred Barnett, Edwin Pitts, Clyde Scott and Steve Van Buren?

8. Billy Ray Barnes, Ed Bawel, Ron Blye and Bob Brown all had alliterative "B" nicknames. What were they?

9. Who were the Dutchman, the Sheriff, the Baron, the Blade, Gummy, the Swamp Fox and Cheewah? How about the Polish Rifle, Big Foot, Big Daddy, Home Boy and the Frito Bandito?

10. What were the real names of Buddy Ryan, Bucko Kilroy, Duce Staley, Smiley Creswell, Buck Shaw, Sonny Jurgensen and Bosh Pritchard?

 OVERTIME: *Uniform Number Question:* 45 was the first number worn by which two Eagles who went into broadcasting?

FAMILY CONNECTIONS

THERE HAVE BEEN 36 EAGLES WITH BROTHERS who've played in the NFL. In some cases there have been multiple brothers: Wilbert Montgomery, Brian Baldinger, Lane Howell, Al Chesley and Luis Zendejas all had two NFL brothers. Some brother combinations are not so obvious, such as Turkey Joe Jones who was the half brother of the Redskins' Charley Taylor. Seven Eagles have had sons follow them into pro football and 14 Eagles were taking after their fathers who played in the league before them.

1. What coach's nephew played for him on the Eagles?
2. Who are the only quarterback brothers ever to be on the roster of the same NFL team in the same season?
3. What other pair of brothers played together on the Eagles?
4. What Eagle center's grandfather played in the NFL in 1931?
5. What Eagle center had a twin brother who played in the NFL?
6. What two linemen who were brothers played together in Washington after one was traded from Philadelphia?
7. The Eagles drafted two brothers from Duke in successive seasons: in the first round in 1940 and in the 16th round in 1941. The brother they picked in 1940 they traded away, and he went on to have a Hall of Fame career. The brother they kept from 1941 wore 40 in his one uninspiring year in the NFL. Who were these brothers?
8. What three Eagle kickers have had brother kickers in the NFL?
9. What Eagle who led the NFL in receptions had a son who played pro football and who fully lived up to his crazy last name?
10. What Eagle quarterback was following in the footsteps of his brother and father by playing pro football?

OVERTIME: *Uniform Number Question:* What burned slice of bread wore 46 for the Eagles?

BIG HITS AND HITTERS

THERE IS NOTHING EAGLE FANS ENJOY MORE than a big hit so thunderous that we can feel it in the stands. The players we root for the most tend to be the hardest hitters, primarily on defense. With special fondness we remember defensive linemen Bucko Kilroy, Claude Humphrey, Big Daddy Hairston, Jerome Brown, Clyde Simmons and Reggie White; linebackers Chuck Bednarik, Maxie Baughan, Bill Bergey, Seth Joyner and Jeremiah Trotter; and defensive backs Tom Brookshier, Irv Cross, Nate Ramsey, Andre Waters, Wes Hopkins and Brian Dawkins. Here are some of the greatest hits in Eagle history.

1. Pittsburgh and Philadelphia were violent rivals in the 1950s. Evidence of this took place in 1954 when Steeler quarterback Jim Finks had his jaw broken by what Eagle pass rush master?

2. In the opening game of the 1953 season against San Francisco, undersized 49er hit man Hardy Brown took out what Eagle runner?

3. Writer and Giants fan Frederick Exley described the tackler in this famous hit as "bearing down like a tractor trailer on a blind man." Who were the principals involved in this on-field traffic accident?

4. The October 24, 1955 issue of *Life* magazine featured a photo essay called "Savagery on Sundays" that decried the prevalence of violence in the NFL. In the piece, Bucko Kilroy was described as the "toughest" and "orneriest" of the roughnecks in the league. How did the magazine illustrate how ornery Kilroy was?

5. On September 26, 1971, Mel Tom applied a shot to the back of Roger Staubach's head as he lay on the ground and knocked him out of the game in the first quarter. How much was Tom fined by the league?

6. In a *Monday Night Football* home opener against the Cowboys in 1974, Bill Bergey made an impact in his first game as an Eagle. His most memorable hit was on Doug Dennison, causing a fumble that was recovered by whom? What happened in the game?

7. How many Redskins did the Eagles knock out of the "Body Bag Game"?

8. Who applied the hit on Luis Zendejas in the "Bounty Bowl"?

9. Whose shoulders did Clyde Simmons and Hugh Douglas separate in games 12 years apart?

10. What ex-Eagle did Jeremiah Trotter send flying in the 2004 opener against the Giants?

 OVERTIME: *Uniform Number Question:* Only one player has worn 47 for more than one year in Philadelphia. Who was this feisty free agent safety who wore it for two seasons?

TRIVIA QUIZ

FIGHTS ON AND OFF THE FIELD

SOMETIMES THOSE BIG HITS that Eagles are known for and that their fans so relish spill over into full-blown fistfights. These fights have occurred during games, after games, in the locker room and in the stands. Most were harmless and comical, but some have been quite serious and bloody.

1. Bucko Kilroy was caught kicking Ray Bray of the Bears in the groin in a 1940s exhibition game. He was fined $150, but the fine was later rescinded. Why?

2. In 1952, Bucko kicked a Cardinal Hall of Famer and was penalized. Moreover, after the game, a few Cardinals waited for Kilroy and began beating him with their helmets as he left the field. What Hall of Fame teammate were they sticking up for?

3. Chuck Bednarik got into more than one fight in the heat of a ballgame, but in 1956, he took that a step further and had a postgame punch-out with what Cleveland Brown messenger guard who would go on to become a Hall of Fame coach?

4. On October 30, 1949, several fights broke out in a game between the Eagles and Steelers. How did one fight have its origins in the Ivy League?

5. Another Eagle who got ejected more than once for fighting in the 1950s was an undersized tight end. Who was he?

6. On November 9, 1953, Norm Willey and the Giants' John Rapacz were ejected in a game in which there were several fights. How did

the Philly fans in Connie Mack Stadium that day react?

7. The most brutal and famous fight in team history happened off the field the day after John F. Kennedy was assassinated. Who were the two Eagles who got hurt in this fight?

8. The 700 level at the Vet had a well-deserved reputation as Philadelphia's version of Fight Club. What was the result of the "Flare Gun Game" against San Francisco on *Monday Night Football* in November 1997?

9. 2005 got off to an ominous start when Jeremiah Trotter was ejected before the opener for taunting, not even fighting, what Falcon?

10. The T.O. saga of 2005 reached a bizarre turn when he got into a fight with what club official in the locker room?

 OVERTIME: *Uniform Number Question: Uniform Number Question:* 48 was worn by what local fullback known for his "horns"?

——— TRIVIA QUIZ 49 ———
ILLEGAL EAGLES

AT TIMES, SOME EAGLES HAVE STRAYED onto the wrong side of the law and have had to pay for their indiscretions, large or small. While some of these stories are simply amusing or colorful, others are much more serious, involving drugs, sexual assault, violence and death. Sadly, a few Eagles made some very bad choices and ruined or ended their lives.

1. Among Alabama Pitts, Nate Ramsey and Roy Barni, who was the luckiest Eagle?

2. Where did Don MacGregor last play before trying out for the Eagles in 1943?

3. The Eagles had a tackle named Jack Dempsey in the 1930s who was sent to prison 30 years later for what crime?

4. Which of these three Eagles won a lawsuit against the team: Don Chuy, Ed Harris or Reggie White?

5. What two Eagles sued *Life* magazine for slander? Who won?

6. Although neither was convicted, two running backs arrested in a drug case were immediately cut by Dick Vermeil in 1978. Who were they?

7. What former Eagle went to prison for rape? What practice squad player was accused of rape before a playoff game, cut from the team and then later convicted of manslaughter in Mississippi?

8. What sidelined the careers of Bernard Williams, Alonzo Johnson and Terrence Carroll?

9. What happened to the wife of Blenda Gay after she was convicted of killing her husband in 1976?

10. Donovan McNabb and Jeremiah Trotter were convicted of what heinous crime in 2006?

 OVERTIME: *Uniform Number Question:* 49 was worn by what halfback who played on both sides of the ball and later coached the team?

TRIVIA QUIZ

INJURIES, BAD LUCK AND
WHAT MIGHT HAVE BEEN

THE MOST DISCOURAGING THING in watching football is when a player gets injured. Football is a rugged game and injuries are bound to happen, but it is always distressing when it does. The current game is not as rough as it was in the 1950s in some ways—there are fewer fights, the players wear facemasks, massive pileups are rare, and clothesline and necktie tackles are illegal. However, the players are faster, bigger and stronger and the equipment is harder, so the high-speed collisions can be brutal and career-ending. Some very talented Eagles have been forced to leave the field well before they had lost their skills.

1. What All-Pro receiver broke his ankle one year, had knee problems the next and leg problems the year after that to end his career?

2. What quarterback had his shoulder separated severely in an exhibition game and was never again the same player for the Eagles?

3. What defensive back suffered a broken leg during a game in which the bone broke through the skin?

4. Who was the quarterback who injured his knee on opening day and then broke his leg in the fourth game two years later?

5. What safety tore up his knee so badly in tackling a former teammate that he wouldn't return for two years?

6. After suffering through two years of foot injuries, what running back suffered a knee injury so grotesque in training camp that his position coach threw up on the field?

7. What safety tore his ACL (anterior cruciate ligament) just as he was starting to come on as a player and had everything spiral out of control afterwards?

8. What defensive tackle signed a $7.5 million contract extension before tearing up his knee in the preseason and was forced to retire the following season after several unsuccessful tries to return?

9. What Eagle missed 35 games due to foot and other injuries over three seasons and then left the team as a free agent to lead the NFL in a major category in 2005?

10. What Eagle had his number retired the season after his tragic accidental death?

 OVERTIME: *Uniform Number Question:* What former Eagle starting middle linebacker who wore 50 moved on to the XFL?

T.O. AND OTHER NONCONFORMISTS

EAGLES WITH PERSONALITIES so big that they have trouble fitting into a team come in a variety of types. They can be loudmouths, egotists and malcontents, or intense leaders or freewheeling, fun-loving flakes. Their effect on the team can be as positive as a Tommy McDonald keeping everyone loose or as negative as a selfish Terrell Owens tearing a team apart. What they all have in common is that they attract attention, are a magnet for television cameras, sell newspapers and keep fans talking and interested. They also tend to drive coaches crazy.

1. Of whom did Terrell Owens say, "Like my boy tells me: 'If it looks like a rat and smells like a rat, by golly, it's a rat'"?

2. What Eagle star runner was suspended for one game as a rookie and again after the fourth game of his fourth year? He never played in Philadelphia again.

3. What Eagle drove an Aston Martin sports car like James Bond and was best known for his unsnapped chinstrap?

4. Who was the Eagle runner who had his girlfriend yell at his position coach because he wanted the ball more?

5. What Eagle left training camp three times in one month?

6. What Eagle chewed glass, set his hair on fire and drove a motorbike off a pier?

7. What disgruntled Eagle cleaned out his locker near the end of the season and wore his team jacket inside out on the sidelines of a game?

8. What linebacker regularly criticized the coach's calls, questioned his guts and called him a puppet without being disciplined?

9. What Eagle would celebrate touchdowns with back flips?

10. What Eagle changed the spelling of his name three times in four years?

 OVERTIME: *Uniform Number Question:* 51 was worn by what college safety who was switched to linebacker in Philadelphia and became an All-Pro?

TRIVIA QUIZ 52
COLLEGES

PLAYERS TAKE GREAT PRIDE in the exploits of their alma maters, even if they didn't graduate. Several Eagles have come from college football factories such as Miami, Florida State, Nebraska, Oklahoma and Notre Dame, but some pretty good as well as pretty obscure Eagles have come from many other schools, even northeastern ones.

1. These Eagles all attended the same college as what prominent Eagle quarterback: Henry Piro, Jack Hinkle, Jim Ringo and Stan Walters?

2. What football powerhouse did L.J. Smith, Nick Prisco and Mike McMahon attend?

3. What college did these three Eagle receivers attend: Kenny Jackson, Scott Fitzkee and Gregg Garrity?

4. These Eagles all chose to go to what local school: Bucko Kilroy, Mike Jarmoluk, Wayne Colman, Hank Reese, Swede Hanson and Dave Smukler?

5. What two small urban colleges do these Eagles hail from: Ted Laux, John Cole, Mike Mandarino, George Somers and Vince Papale?

6. These Eagles all went to the same school as what Philadelphia game-breaker: Nick Basca, Dave DiFillipo, Frank Budd, Billy Walik, Kevin Reilly and Brian Finneran?

7. These Eagles all attended the same highly respected school as what World War II waist gunner and versatile Bird: Ed Bell, Frank Reagan, Fran Murray, Diddy Willson and George Savitsky?

8. What suburban college that doubled as a training camp site did these Eagles attend: John Ferko, Merritt Kersey, Carl Gersbach and Chuck Weber?

9. What do the schools that Lane Howell, Woody Peoples, Andre Waters and Carl Hairston attended have in common?

10. What is the common thread running through the college choice of these Eagles: Alabama Pitts, Carl Fagioli, Duke Maronic, Danny DiRenzo, Don Clayton, Dick Hart, Dick Lachman, Ted Wegert and Jack Ferrante?

 OVERTIME: *Uniform Number Question:* What center who wore 52 didn't make the NFL till he was 29 and didn't make All-Pro till he was 37?

MISCELLANEOUS

THIS IS THE QUIZ where I fit in some questions that didn't fit anywhere else. Several are related to Eagles who served in the military and the rest are mostly about Eagles who had a baseball connection.

1. What guard lost part of his arm on Iwo Jima and played for the Eagles afterwards?
2. Who were the two Eagles who lost their lives in World War II?
3. What Eagle head coaches served during the Korean War?
4. What Eagle owners served in a world war?
5. What Eagle head coaches served in World War II?
6. What 1960s linebacker served in the Army before attending college?
7. What Eagles linebacker lost an arm to cancer?
8. What former Eagles beat reporter pitched for the Phillies and the A's?
9. What former Penn athlete pitched for the Phillies, the A's and the Senators and played in the backfield for the 1936 Eagles?
10. What former Penn multi-sport star became the first athlete to play major league baseball and NFL football in the same year?

OVERTIME: *Uniform Number Question:* What linebacker who wore 53 for the Eagles played in Super Bowls for San Francisco, Denver and Oakland?

SECTION VI
RECORDS

TRIVIA QUIZ 54

GAME RECORDS

OFTEN WHAT WE FANS REMEMBER most are individual games in which a player or players did something really special on the field. In many cases, we remember the big hits in Philly, but we also remember achievements that can be better measured by statistics. Some record-setting achievements were positive and some were negative, but all occupy way too much space in our Eagle-addled brains.

1. What two Eagles rushed for over 200 yards in a game?
2. What two Eagles carried the ball the most times in a game?
3. Who was the first Eagle to score four touchdowns in a game?
4. Who was the coach when the Eagles set their all-time team record for rushing yards in a game?
5. What Eagle scored the most points in one game?
6. Who was the coach when the Eagles set their all-time team record for total yards in a game?
7. What Eagle attempted the most passes in a game?
8. Donovan McNabb's 464 yards passing against the Packers in 2004 broke whose team record?
9. What two Eagle quarterbacks share the team record with six interceptions in a game?
10. Who was the coach when the Eagles set their all-time record for penalty yards in a game?

 OVERTIME: *Uniform Number Question:* Buddy Ryan traded seven draft picks to the Bears for the draft rights to what Eagles special teams MVP?

TRIVIA QUIZ 55

SEASONAL RECORDS

EAGLE PLAYERS HAVE HAD SOME great seasons over the years and posted some remarkable numbers. Looking through the seasonal records brings to mind many great Eagle performers from the past and highlights some exciting and memorable seasons in team history.

1. In what year did the Eagles score the most points? In what year did they average the most points per game?
2. What Eagle kicked the most extra points in one season?
3. What Eagle scored the most touchdowns rushing in a season? How many?
4. What Eagle threw the most touchdown passes in a season? How many?
5. What Eagle threw the most interceptions in a season? How many?
6. What Eagle running back caught the most passes in a season? How many?
7. What Eagle intercepted the most passes in a season? How many?
8. What Eagle scored the most touchdowns on defense in a season?
9. What Eagle holds the record for kickoff return yards in a season?
10. What Eagle holds the record for most punt return yards in a season?

 OVERTIME: *Uniform Number Question:* 55 was worn by what rookie starter on the 1960 champions who went to the Pro Bowl in every Eagle season but one?

TRIVIA QUIZ 56

CAREER RECORDS

ASIDE FROM REGGIE WHITE, there are no Eagles listed among the all-time NFL leaders in any major career category. While Steve Van Buren was once the league's all-time leading rusher, that was a long time ago. Nevertheless, Eagle career leaders have achieved some impressive cumulative numbers that stand as markers for future Birds to exceed.

1. Who threw the most touchdown passes as an Eagle? Whose career touchdown pass record did he break?

2. Who was the first Eagle quarterback to reach 100 interceptions?

3. Wilbert Montgomery passed Steve Van Buren in 1983 as the all-time Eagles rushing leader. Who held the record before Van Buren?

4. Who punted the ball more than any other Eagle?

5. Whose Eagle career sack record did Reggie White break? When?

6. Randall Cunningham holds the team record for yards rushing by a quarterback with 4,482. Whose team record did he break?

7. Who scored the most touchdowns as an Eagle?

8. When did Bobby Walston become the all-time leading Eagles scorer? Whose record did he break?

9. Who played the most games in an Eagle uniform? Who played the most seasons in an Eagle uniform?

10. Who lost the most games as an Eagle head coach?

 OVERTIME: *Uniform Number Question:* 56 was worn by what linebacker who turned down a contract extension in 1994 and then broke his leg and tore up his knee on the same tackle and never played again?

TRIVIA QUIZ 57

ROOKIES

EACH YEAR AT DRAFT TIME, Eagle fans get excited about who the Eagles may select. Sometimes they are displeased, such as when a group of Eagle fans in the audience at the draft booed when Donovan McNabb was announced as the Eagles' first choice in 1999 rather than fan favorite Ricky Williams. Fans don't always know best. However, no matter what player the Eagles take, it reignites the excitement of the new. A rookie is a blank slate with unlimited potential until he steps on the field and shows himself to be a human being with both talents and flaws.

1. What Eagle led the NFL in receiving as a rookie?
2. What Eagle running back scored on a run from scrimmage, a punt return and a kickoff return as a rookie?
3. Who holds the team record for rushing yards by a rookie?
4. What rookie led the league in passing yards?
5. What Eagle rookies were starters on defending championship teams?
6. What two defensive backs share the record for most interceptions by a rookie?
7. Who holds the Eagle rookie scoring record?
8. What Eagle rookie guard was named All-Pro wearing the same number later retired for Chuck Bednarik?
9. Who holds the Eagle rookie record for most yards passing?
10. What Eagle rookie receiver caught the most touchdown passes?

OVERTIME: *Uniform Number Question:* 57 was worn by what former Cowboy whose father played 16 years with the New England Patriots?

TRIVIA QUIZ 58

AWARDS

FOOTBALL IS NOT THE MOVIES, and there are no Oscars for the sport. The one award every football player wants most is the Super Bowl ring of a champion, but the media and different organizations give out some awards as well. Eagle players have won each of the major awards at least once.

1. What five Eagle coaches have won Coach of the Year? Which one won it twice?
2. Which coach was fired the fastest after winning the award?
3. Who is the only tight end ever to win an NFL MVP Award?
4. What three other Eagles have won league MVP awards? Who won it twice as an Eagle?
5. What Eagle has been named defensive MVP of the league? How many times?
6. What three Eagles have won Comeback Player of the Year?
7. What Eagle was given an award that was inscribed, "To the greatest player of all time. Small in stature with the heart of a lion. A living inspiration to the youth of America"?
8. What Eagle was named All-Pro the most times? How many times?
9. Who was named to the Pro Bowl the most times as an Eagle? How many times?
10. No Eagle has worn more than two championship rings with Philadelphia. What Eagles have won more than two Super Bowl rings? What Eagles have won more than two NFL championships?

 OVERTIME: *Uniform Number Question:* 58 was the first number worn by what Hawaiian defensive end who later shifted to 99?

TRIVIA QUIZ 59

HONOR ROLL

THE EAGLES HONOR ROLL was established in 1987 to pay tribute to outstanding members of the organization. In 1987, 13 men were inducted. Since then, 14 men and two teams have followed. However, the last inductions to the Honor Roll were in 1999. Under Jeff Lurie, the Eagles seem to have lost interest in this salute to Eagles tradition, which is surprising since there are ways they could make money off of it. If the Eagles made their Honor Roll inductions a more regular occurrence and had a formal dinner for which fans could buy tickets to commemorate great Eagles of the past, there would be considerable local interest and money could be raised for the team's charitable programs. The Packers do this with their team Hall of Fame, and it seems to be a very popular event and attraction. It is a great way to honor players who served the team and its fans well, but who were not at a Hall of Fame level.

1. Who has been honored since Jeff Lurie bought the franchise?
2. What three quarterbacks are honored?
3. What three centers are honored?
4. Who are the four honorees who played under Joe Kuharich?
5. What honoree was with the team for the longest time?
6. What honoree spent the shortest time in Philadelphia?
7. What three coaches are honored?
8. What pair of tackles is honored?
9. What six receivers are honored?
10. Are more individuals honored from the 1948-49 champs, the 1960 champs or the 1980 Super Bowl team?

 OVERTIME: *Uniform Number Question:* Who replaced Hall of Fame center Jim Ringo at center for the Eagles and wore 59?

TRIVIA QUIZ 60

THE HALL OF FAME

To date **16 former Eagles** have been inducted into the Pro Football Hall of Fame in Canton, Ohio. With 16 inductees, the Eagles are tied with the Lions for 9th in number of Hall of Famers. Of those 16, nine are considered primarily Eagles, and in this category, the Birds are tied for 13th with the Dolphins and Cowboys. Of the eight NFL franchises at least as old as the Eagles, only the Cardinals have fewer Hall of Famers and none has fewer primary Hall of Famers. A good case could be made for such Eagles as eight-time All-Pro tackle Al Wistert, seven-time All-Pro Bucko Kilroy and receiver Harold Carmichael deserving consideration for the Hall.

1. Reggie White will be inducted into the Hall of Fame posthumously in 2006. What previous Eagles were inducted after their death?

2. Who is the Eagle Hall of Famer with the least connection to the team?

3. What two Eagles did Greasy Neale present at their induction ceremonies?

4. Who presented Greasy Neale at his induction?

5. Why did Steve Van Buren choose Packer Hall of Famer Clarke Hinkle to present him at his induction?

6. What sportswriter who won the Dick McCann Award for "long and distinguished reporting in the field of pro football" and a spot on the Writer's Honor Roll in Canton presented Tommy McDonald?

7. What three Eagle Hall of Famers never played for any other team?

8. What five representatives from the 1948 and/or 1949 championship teams are in the Hall of Fame?

9. What four representatives from the 1960 championship team are in the Hall of Fame?

10. What six Eagle Hall of Famers are not in the College Football Hall of Fame in South Bend, Indiana? These six include a coach, a center, a runner, a passer and two receivers.

 OVERTIME: *Uniform Number Question:* Who was the last Eagle to wear 60 before Chuck Bednarik?

Quiz
Answers

QUIZ ANSWERS !!!!

SECTION I
HISTORY

EAGLE PREHISTORY

1. A year after the Philadelphia Football Club was formed in 1901, Hall of Fame baseball manager Connie Mack started the football Athletics to compete with them, but Connie's team only lasted a season and went 3-2-1.

2. Blue Laws in Philadelphia prohibited football from being played on Sundays, so the Yellow Jackets would typically try to schedule a home-and-home weekend series with an opposing team—a game in Frankford on Saturday followed by a train ride and a game in the opponent's town on Sunday.

3. Hust Stockton was a star runner and passer for Frankford from 1925 to 1928. He attended Gonzaga as did his grandson John who was a perennial All-NBA selection at point guard for the Utah Jazz and was selected as one of the 50 Greatest NBA Players of All Time in 1996.

4. Henry "Two Bits" Homan from Lebanon Valley College played for Frankford from 1925 to 1930. Despite his small stature, he averaged over 13 yards per punt return. He also caught the TD pass that beat the Bears to clinch the title in 1926.

5. Guy Chamberlin from Nebraska played for the NFL champion Chicago Staleys under George Halas in 1921, moved on to become player-coach of the champion Canton Bulldogs in 1922 and 1923 and the champion Cleveland Bulldogs in 1924. He was player-coach of Frankford in 1925-26 and again won the league title in 1926. That's five NFL titles in six years. This one-man dynasty finished his career as both a player and coach with the Chicago Cardinals in 1927, but even he couldn't produce a title for the Cardinals.

6. Despite having the best record in the NFL in 1925, Pottsville was suspended from the league and the Chicago Cardinals bypassed them for the championship. The instigation for the suspension was that Pottsville played an unauthorized exhibition game against a team of Notre Dame All-Stars in another team's territory. The game was played in November in Philadelphia, Frankford's territory.

7. Both the Yellow Jackets and Quakers won the championship of their respective leagues. The Quakers challenged the Yellow Jackets to a playoff, but were refused. Instead, the Quakers played the seventh-place Giants and lost 31-0.

8. Tackle Joe Carpe played two games for the brand new Eagles in 1933. In the 1920s, he played for both the NFL champion Frankford Yellow Jackets and the Pottsville Maroons.

9. The stadium burned down in 1931, so the team had to play on several different fields that season, their last before going out of business.

10. Although Bert Bell, Lud Wray and their investors had to pay off Frankford's $25,000 in debts, the franchise they were awarded by the league was considered a brand-new one.

OVERTIME: *Uniform Number Question:* Woeful kicker Happy Feller wore 1 in 1971. He connected on only six of 20 field goal attempts and was cut.

QUIZ ANSWERS

THE 1930s

1. On October 16, 1933, the Eagles were crushed 56-0 by the New York Giants at the Polo Grounds. It is still the worst loss ever suffered by the team.

2. Swede Hanson, the team's first star, appropriately scored first on a 35-yard touchdown pass from Roger Kirkman on October 29, 1933 in a loss to Green Bay in the third game of the season.

3. Bert Bell's Penn teammate, Lud Wray, was his ownership partner and coached the team in its first three seasons. His record was 9-21-1.

4. On November 5, 1933, the Eagles won 6-0 over the Cincinnati Reds in Cincinnati. Swede Hanson scored the only TD.

5. The week before, the city's Blue Laws prohibiting Sunday sports were struck down. The Eagles drew a capacity crowd of 20,000 for the city's first professional Sunday game and they tied the Bears 3-3.

6. The opener against the Steelers was postponed till Thanksgiving due to "threatening weather" on a day when the baseball Athletics played a doubleheader seven blocks away because Bert Bell realized he wouldn't draw much of a crowd competing with baseball.

7. On November 6, 1934, the Eagles buried the Cincinnati Reds 64-0 with both Swede Hanson and Joe Carter scoring three touchdowns. It was the Reds' last game ever; they were absorbed by the semi-pro St. Louis Gunners who then replaced them in the NFL for the rest of the season.

8. Tackle/kicker Hank Reese led the team with nine points on two field goals and three extra points.

9. It was the first NFL game ever televised, albeit to an audience of roughly 500 TV receivers in the New York area. Allen Waltz called the game that was broadcast by just two cameras. The game drew a crowd of 13,000, and the Dodgers won 23-14. That was not the

Birds' first experience with television, though. Five years earlier, the Eagles had taken part in a demonstration of television at the Franklin Institute during one of their practices.

10. Sadly, that was the only time the Eagles' all-time won-lost record stood at .500. They lost the last two games of 1933 and have been under .500 ever since.

OVERTIME: *Uniform Number Question:* End Joe Pilconis from Temple wore 2, 18, 24 and 28 in his three years with the Eagles, mostly as a backup. He coached high school football in Pennsylvania for several years.

QUIZ ANSWERS

THE 1940s

1. With Davey O'Brien at tailback, the Eagles passed the ball 362 times while only rushing it 317.

2. Pittsburgh owner Art Rooney and Bert Bell were struggling in 1940 and originally proposed to merge as the only way to improve the quality of their clubs. Instead, 26-year-old millionaire Lex Thompson purchased the Pittsburgh franchise from Rooney, and Rooney bought 50% of the Eagles from Bell. Existing players were shifted between the two teams. Thompson intended to keep his team in Pittsburgh for only a season and then move them to Boston so he could be closer to his New York business headquarters. Rooney and Bell planned to rename their team the Pennsylvania Keystoners, who would operate out of both Philadelphia and Pittsburgh after Thompson moved. By spring 1941, though, Rooney was homesick for Pittsburgh and so the two entities swapped cities. Lex Thompson now owned the new Philadelphia Eagles, and Art Rooney, along with Bert Bell, was back in Pittsburgh with the new Steelers. The new Steelers went from two wins in 1940 to one win in 1941, while the new Eagles went from one win in 1940 to two wins in 1941.

3. Two. Former Pittsburgh Pirate Tommy Thompson became the star quarterback of the Eagles, and Pittsburgh draft pick Vic Sears would be a stalwart Eagle tackle for 13 years.

4. Neale switched from the Single Wing Offense to the T-Formation that the Bears used to destroy the Redskins 73-0 in the 1940 title game.

5. They merged with Pittsburgh to form the Philadelphia-Pittsburgh Eagles-Steelers, known as the Steagles. Greasy Neale handled the offense and Steeler coach Walt Kiesling the defense, the only time two Hall of Famers co-coached an NFL team.

6. This is a trick question. The Steagles finished with a positive 5-4-1 in 1943, but the first time the Eagles alone had a winning season was 1944 with 7-1-1. 1944 was Steve Van Buren's rookie year.

7. 45-0. What a team they were. The Eagles also beat Washington 42-21 and Detroit 45-21 that year and scored more than 30 points in three other games. So in eight of their 12 games in 1948, the Eagles exceeded 30 points. Greasy Neale's offense was high-powered. In 1947, they scored over 30 three times and over 40 three more times, while in 1949, they scored in the 30s four times and in the 40s three times. Summing up, in the 36 regular season games from 1947 to 1949, Philadelphia scored at least 30 points 21 times, or 58% of the time.

8. Neale's alignment has been described alternately as a 7-4, 7-2-2, 5-4-2 and 5-2-4. Along the front line it featured two ends, two tackles and a middle guard. In between the end and the tackle on each side was a linebacker. The new four-man defensive backfield consisted of two defensive halfbacks out on the wings a few yards back and two safeties deep in the middle. The responsibility of the five linemen was to stop the run and rush the passer; the linebackers were lined up over the two offensive ends and were charged with chucking those ends so they could not get into the secondary quickly or easily.

9. Cardinal All-Pro tackle Stan Mauldin had a heart attack and died in the locker room.

10. Hall of Fame runner Steve Van Buren with 402 points.

 OVERTIME: *Uniform Number Question:* Roger "Red" Kirkman wore both 3 and 19 as an Eagle and threw the first Eagle TD pass in their third game against the Packers in 1933.

 QUIZ ANSWERS

THE 1950s

1. Some call the 1950 showdown between the four-time All-America Conference champion Browns and the two-time NFL champion Eagles the first Super Bowl game. The two leagues had battled for players and fans in an expensive, four-year war before finally merging in 1950. The Browns were one of three teams, along with the 49ers and the original Baltimore Colts, to be absorbed into the older league. In setting up the schedule for the season, Commissioner Bert Bell saw an opportunity for optimum exposure for

professional football and arranged for the Browns to meet the Eagles in Philadelphia's massive Municipal Stadium on a Saturday night opening game for the NFL season. Unfortunately, it was a one-sided competition with the Browns winning 35-10. Throughout the '50s and '60s, the Browns and Eagles were fierce rivals and played many games marred by violence, but Cleveland went 26-10-1 versus the Birds in that period.

2. Chuck Bednarik played in 119 of the Eagles' 120 games during the decade.

3. "The Sheriff" Bobby Walston scored 631 points kicking and receiving.

4. In 1952, halfbacks Ralph Goldston, an 11th-round draft pick, and Don Stevens, a 30th-round choice, each made the team. Neither would last more than three seasons in the NFL.

5. Guard Ray Romero was a free agent from Kansas State who started seven games in 1951 as a rookie. The Mexican-American then went into the service and never returned to the NFL.

6. Bo McMillin, who had coached Eagle end Pete Pihos at Indiana University, was hired to replace Greasy Neale in 1951. After winning the first two games of the season, McMillan was forced to step down due to cancer. He died the next year.

7. They both played for Notre Dame under Knute Rockne. Devore was fired in 1958 after compiling a 7-16-1 record in two seasons as the Eagles' coach. Shaw was hired as his replacement.

8. New York Giants offensive coach Vince Lombardi was offered the job by GM Vince McNally, but was advised by Giants owner Wellington Mara to refuse it due to the unstable ownership situation of the Eagles.

9. Bell verbally promised Van Brocklin the coaching job once Buck Shaw stepped down. After the Eagles won the title in 1960 and Shaw retired, Van Brocklin was furious that the Eagles were not interested in him as coach. By then, Bell was dead, so Van Brocklin took the head coaching job in Minnesota.

10. In 1957, the first four rounds went (1) Clarence Peaks, (2) Billy Barnes, (3) Tommy McDonald and (4) Sonny Jurgensen; the Eagles had filled a complete backfield in one draft.

 OVERTIME: *Uniform Number Question:* In his first game as an Eagle, Dale Dawson missed a fourth-quarter, 22-yard field goal on September 26, 1988 in a 23-21 loss to Minnesota; Buddy Ryan cut him that week.

QUIZ ANSWERS 5

THE 1960s

1. The Eagles got blown out by Cleveland at home. Instead of losing 35-10, they lost 41-24. Few expected they would win their next nine games, including a thrilling 31-29 comeback win in Cleveland four weeks later, and win a title.

2. Bob Pelegrini went down in the fifth game of the year (the comeback victory noted above), causing coach Buck Shaw to use Bednarik on both offense and defense for the next few weeks.

3. Pete Retzlaff broke his arm in the fourth game of the year. Tight end Bobby Walston also broke his that year, although he continued to kick for the team and didn't miss a game. Retzlaff returned for the last four games of the season, playing a new position, tight end, with a cast on his arm.

4. The Eagles finished second in the East in 1961 and thus went on to play in the meaningless Runner-Up Bowl against the Lions the week after the championship game. After throwing an interception, Sonny Jurgensen was blocked into the ground by Wayne Walker on the return. Jurgensen suffered what the team doctor referred to as the worst shoulder separation he had ever seen. Sonny would not be the same for a couple more years.

5. Another theory for the decline of Sonny Jurgensen in 1962-63 is that his favorite coach, Charlie Gauer, left the team to attend to business concerns. By the time Gauer returned to the team, Jurgensen was gone. Gauer served the Eagles for many years as a player, assistant coach, scout and broadcaster.

6. After having lost to the Cowboys 56-7 four weeks before in Dallas, Philadelphia won this game on two Timmy Brown kickoff returns for TDs and a 67-yard punt return TD by Aaron Martin, the lone bright spot in his career in Philadelphia. The game was saved at the end when Joe Scarpatti stripped Dan Reeves of the ball deep in Eagle territory.

7. Bobby Shann returned his first punt 63 yards for a TD in 1965, but was injured and didn't play again till 1967 when he returned three more punts for 17 total yards.

8. In 1968, when O.J. Simpson was a senior in college, the Eagles lost the first 11 games of the year. Out of nowhere, they muscled up two straight wins (12-0 over Detroit and 29-17 over the Saints) before losing the last game and finishing 2-12. Buffalo aced them out for Simpson and the Eagles selected two-way back Leroy Keyes from Purdue who had injury problems and never fulfilled his potential. Also available at their draft slot was Mean Joe Greene.

9. Jerry Williams, who had played halfback and defensive back for the Birds in the 1950s and had served as their defensive coach in 1960 before becoming a head coach in Canada. Williams lasted little more than two years with a 7-22-2 record.

10. Founder and coach Bert Bell, although he was voted in largely for his contributions as commissioner.

OVERTIME: *Uniform Number Question:* Roman Gabriel couldn't wear his familiar 18 until Ben Hawkins was traded, so for 1973 he wore 5.

QUIZ ANSWERS

THE 1970s

1. Both the players and the owner are correct here. After losing the first three games of 1971 by 23, 35 and 28 points, Williams fined several players for lack of effort. However, when owner Len Tose went to Williams and asked him to step down, Williams refused and was fired. Jerry publicly berated the owner: "Unfortunately, I was working for a man without courage or character. I was offered a sizeable sum of money to resign, but to accept a bribe of that nature is to lower myself to his depths."

2. All players had to shave their facial hair because "Good grooming is one of the many facets of discipline."

3. The free-spirited teammates and defensive leaders spent their 17-day holdout working out at the beach along the Jersey Shore. When the smoke cleared, defending NFL interception leader Bradley was signed, and Rossovich was traded to San Diego.

4. At 6'5", quarterback Roman Gabriel brought a passing attack back to Philadelphia when he was acquired in 1973. His tall targets included 6'4" tight end Charles Young, 6'4" wide out Don Zimmerman and 6'8" wide out Harold Carmichael.

5. McCormack had also coached under George Allen and tried to rebuild the Eagles quickly by trading draft choices for veterans like Allen did in Washington, but aside from picking up Gabriel, Stan Walters and Bill Bergey, most of his acquisitions were of the much lower caliber of Norm Bulaich, Mike Boryla, Jerry Patton and John Tarver. Both the present and future of the team were devastated.

6. In the first season of *Monday Night Football* during a 23-20 Eagle win over the Giants, Cosell had to leave at halftime after throwing up on Don Meredith's shoes. He claimed to be sick from running laps with sprinter Tommy Smith before the game. Most speculated that he had been drinking.

7. Wade Key, a third-round pick from Southwest Texas State in 1969 who lasted 10 years in the league, mostly as a starter although never a star. He played in 121 of the Eagles' 144 games in the 1970s.

8. Early in 1972, tight end Fred Hill approached owner Len Tose distraught because his daughter had leukemia. Tose and general manager Jim Murray started a major campaign called the Eagles Fly for Leukemia that goes on to this day. The drive paid for the construction of the oncology unit in Children's Hospital and laboratories in the hospital's Cancer Research Center.

9. Don't be shocked, but it happened in a road game, all you Philly bashers. On October 27, 1974, Saints fans held up the Saints' 14-10 victory over Philadelphia for 18 minutes by booing the officials so loudly that the Eagles could not get off a play. The officials sent both teams to the sidelines and had the band play music in the interim till the fans quieted down. When the teams returned, the Eagles, who had been in Saint territory, lost their momentum and failed to score.

10. Just three. Roman Gabriel led the Eagles over the Cowboys once in 1973 and Bill Bergey keyed a victory in 1974. The third was a very satisfying Monday Night Football win in Dallas, 31-21 in 1979, that signaled Vermeil's Eagles had arrived.

 OVERTIME: *Uniform Number Question:* Bubby Brister played one year under Kotite in New York before dropping out of football for a year. Denver signed him in 1997 to backup John Elway, and he got to two Super Bowls.

QUIZ ANSWERS

THE 1980s

1. A 68-year-old offensive guru of the deep passing offense, Sid Gilman worked as Dick Vermeil's quarterback coach in 1979-80. In those two seasons, Jaworski threw for 45 touchdowns and only 24 interceptions. The previous two seasons, he threw for 34 TDs and 37 picks. In the two years after Gilman left, Jaws threw 35 TDs and 32 interceptions. Marion Campbell brought Gilman back in 1985 to work with Randall Cunningham, but Randall was a less-dedicated pupil than Jaws had been.

2. After having gone to the playoffs the previous four seasons, the Eagles started 1-1 before the 1982 strike. When they returned eight weeks later, they lost to the Bengals

18-14 at home and were roundly booed. To top it off, Leonard Tose came into the locker room after the game and told the players they should have stayed on strike. Bad team chemistry and aging players contributed to a 3-6 finish and Dick Vermeil's tearful, burned-out retirement at the end of the year.

3. The immediate effect was negative in that the Birds lost all three replacement player games, with coach Buddy Ryan clearly not putting out any effort, and finished 7-8. The long-term effect was that the players stuck together and Ryan sided with them over management, forging a permanent bond.

4. Phoenix, who would soon get a different bird team, the Cardinals.

5. Don Shula's son, David. David Shula would become coach of the Cincinnati Bengals seven years later and never achieve a winning season in five years. Since the Braman/Gamble team later picked Rich Kotite over Jeff Fisher, they clearly demonstrated that they were not to be trusted picking coaches.

6. Mike Quick caught a 99-yard TD pass in 1985 against Atlanta in overtime, the equivalent of a "walk off home run" in baseball since it abruptly ended the game.

7. On December 6, 1981, the Eagles trailed the Redskins 15-13 with one minute to play when Ron Jaworski furiously drove the team from his 20 to the Redskins' 7. Tony Franklin came out to attempt the 25-yard chip shot to win the game, but never got the chance because holder John Sciara dropped the snap and was tackled.

8. Although Bob "Boomer" Brown weighed 300 pounds at times in the 1960s, the first Eagle officially listed at 300 was forgettable tackle Frank Giddens in 1981.

9. At 5'8" were returner Wally Henry, runner Alan Reid and defensive back Tom Caterbone; at 5'7" were runner Mark Higgs and kicker David Jacobs; at 5'6" was returner Gizmo Williams. Caterbone and Jacobs were replacement players. The 1990s featured five such players: 5'8" Vaughn Hebron; 5'7" Mark McMillian, Allen Rossum and Eric Bieniemy and 5'6" Jeff Sydnor. The shortest player since then has been Brian Westbrook at 5'8".

10. Ron Baker, obtained from the Colts for an eighth-round draft pick in 1980, appeared in 123 of the Eagles' 152 games in the 1980s.

 OVERTIME: *Uniform Number Question:* The Eagles picked up Roy Zimmerman in 1943 from Washington for Jack Smith and Ken Hayden. He would be their starter for the next three years till Thompson returned and Zimmerman was traded to Detroit.

THE 1990s

1. Bud Carson, who had coached the defenses of both the Steelers and Rams to the Super Bowl in the 1970s. Under Carson, Buddy Ryan's fiery and talented but undisciplined defense became even more dominant.

2. Jeff Fisher, who had played under Buddy in Chicago, was something of a protégé of Ryan, and that didn't help him in competing with Rich Kotite, who had been brought to Philadelphia by Norman Braman and Harry Gamble.

3. Ray Rhodes in 1995 with Jon Gruden as his offensive coordinator. Its emphasis on constant dink-and-dunk passing has never been wholly popular in this blue-collar town that favors a running attack.

4. The "Fourth and One Game." On December 10, 1995, when Switzer had the Cowboys go for a fourth and one at their own 29 with 2:00 remaining and the score tied. They ran Emmitt Smith to the left, and he was stuffed for no gain, but the officials ruled that the two-minute warning had come before the ball was snapped. With the benefit of a do-over, Dallas ran the very same play and they were stuffed again. The Eagles had the ball, kicked a field goal and won 20-17.

5. Mark Bowden, who wrote a terrific book about the 1992 Eagles—*Bringing the Heat*, followed that up with *Black Hawk Down*, a National Book Award finalist in 1999.

6. Clyde Simmons, 44.5 sacks in four seasons; Reggie White, 43 sacks in three seasons; Andy Harmon, 39.5 sacks in seven seasons; William Fuller, 35.5 sacks in three seasons; Willie Thomas, 33 sacks in nine seasons; Mike Mamula, 26 sacks in five seasons; Seth Joyner, 22.5 sacks in four seasons.

7. Herschel Walker rushed for a 91-yard touchdown, caught a pass for 93 yards and returned a kickoff for a 94-yard score all in 1994.

8. After the Eagles lost 20-7 on opening day to the Buccaneers in 1995, new free agent running back Ricky Watters was asked by reporters why he didn't fully extend to try to catch a pass over the middle. His response did not endear him to Eagle fans: "For who? For what?" Although he apologized later, this street version of discretion being the better part of valor never faded away.

9. Ace kick returner Brian Mitchell, who had been a quarterback in college.

10. Handicapped might be a better word. Philadelphia scored just 161 points in 16 games under the drab leadership of Bobby Hoying, Koy Detmer and Rodney Peete. Since 1941, when they instituted the T-Formation, the Eagles have never averaged fewer points per game and have only scored fewer three times: 145 in 14 games in 1972, 134 in 11 games in 1942 and 119 in 11 games in 1941.

OVERTIME: *Uniform Number Question:* 5'7" tailback Davey O'Brien weighed only 150 pounds in 1939-40.

QUIZ ANSWERS 9

THE 2000s

1. Greasy Neale was 63-43-5 as Eagle coach from 1941 to 1950; Reid is 70-42 through 2005. Neale went 3-1 with two titles in the postseason; Reid is 7-5 with none.

2. WIP had dabbled in sports talk previously, but in 1991 Tom Brookshier came in as part owner and collaborator on the morning show with former *Inquirer* sportswriter Angelo Cataldi and the station took on a new vibrancy and harder edge. The generally sensitive Eagles management has never been happy with this situation.

3. The Eagles beat the Giants 24-21 in a close contest that was a defensive struggle for three quarters with New York leading 10-7 before a 28-point explosion in the last quarter. McNabb tied the game with a TD pass at the two-minute mark and led another drive that culminated in a 35-yard David Akers field goal with seven seconds left. After the kickoff, the Giants executed a nearly flawless hook-and-lateral that ended the game when safety Damon Moore at last shoved Ron Dixon out of bounds on the Eagles' 6 yard line with no time remaining.

4. Safety Roy Williams.

5. The Raiders lost the AFC Conference Championship game each year from 1973 to 1975; in 1976 they went to the Super Bowl. The Eagles also lost three straight conference championship games before getting to the Super Bowl the fourth year. However, the Raiders won the Super Bowl that year; the Eagles did not.

6. Brain Dawkins, September 29, 2002, against the Houston Texans.

7. Officially, Tra Thomas at 349 pounds. However, anyone who saw Refrigerator Perry waddling on and off the field in 1993 and 1994 would be shocked if he were less than 400 pounds. More recently, Shawn Andrews was listed at over 370 pounds in college, but the Eagles say he is 340.

8. Brandon Whiting and a fifth-round pick.

9. Four—the maximum—but Owens was made inactive for the remaining five games of the season. He appealed through the union, but lost in a well-publicized hearing with an arbitrator.

10. Jon Runyan has yet to miss a game this decade, 96 straight.

 OVERTIME: *Uniform Number Question:* Joe Pisarcik was the quarterback of the Giants that day and wore 9 when he came to Philadelphia two years later.

QUIZ ANSWERS

THE PLAYING FIELD

1. Baker Bowl was a tiny, dilapidated, deteriorating bandbox in North Philadelphia where the Phillies had played since 1895. Seating capacity was 20,000 and the gridiron just barely fit in between the first-base dugout and the left-field bleachers. The Eagles never drew more than 18,000 fans to any game and averaged less than 10,000 per game there. However, it was the site of both the Eagles' first home game against the Portsmouth Spartans on October 18, 1933 and the first Sunday football game in Philadelphia on November 12, 1933 against the Bears. The Eagles also played two games at Temple Stadium in the 1930s.

2. In 1936, Bert Bell moved the team to cavernous Municipal Stadium in South Philly, and they played there for the rest of the decade. Municipal Stadium, which was renamed JFK Stadium after the Kennedy assassination, was built in 1926 for the city's Sesquicentennial Exposition celebrating the 150th birthday of the nation. It was a giant horseshoe that sat 100,000 people, similar to many college football edifices built around that time. The annual Army-Navy games were played there. The Eagles also played "home" games in Johnstown, Pa.; Erie, Pa.; Charleston, W.V.; Colorado Springs, Co. and Buffalo, N.Y. in the last four years of the decade.

3. The Eagles never drew more than 33,000 in those years and usually drew much less than 20,000. That made the place a giant echo chamber. The biggest two crowds came in the first two games of the 1939 season with attendance of 33,258 against the Redskins and 30,600 against the Giants. These were the first two games of Heisman Trophy winner Davey O'Brien's career, and he had a positive effect on attendance until it became obvious that the team was worse than ever. After 1939, the Eagles played a few more dates in Municipal Stadium, but it would never again be their home.

4. Bell signed a lease with the Philadelphia A's to play in Shibe Park and moved the team back to North Philadelphia in 1940. The Eagles spent the next 18 years in Shibe Park,

seven blocks away from the old Baker Bowl. Once again the gridiron was stretched from the first-base dugout to the left-field area. Temporary unprotected bleachers were erected in right field to boost the capacity to 39,000. Generally, during the championship years of the late 1940s, the Eagles drew from 22,000 to 35,000 fans per home game. The park was later called Connie Mack Stadium and was purchased in the 1960s by Eagles owner Jerry Wolman, even though the football team did not play there.

5. With attendance declining, due partly to external factors such as a rough neighborhood and little parking, the Eagles contracted with the University of Pennsylvania to play at Franklin Field. The rent was higher and the team had to help with the maintenance of the field, but the neighborhood was better, there was more parking and the seating capacity was 68,000. Franklin Field was a ballpark with the shape and sightlines designed expressly for football without being freakishly large; it was horseshoe-shaped with a brick field house at the open end. While it was originally constructed from wood in 1895, it was rebuilt with steel and concrete and a brick exterior in 1922.

6. Attendance jumped 10,000 a game from 22,000 to 32,000. By the next decade attendance was over 60,000 per game and has remained so ever since.

7. $50 million. That's quite a bit more than Franklin Field, but only a tenth of what the Linc would cost 32 years later.

8. Dallas whipped the Eagles 42-7, taking advantage of seven interceptions.

9. The fans began their serenade with a chorus of "Goodbye, Jerry" in honor of the coach. They followed that with a chorus of "Goodbye, Leonard" for the team owner and concluded with "Goodbye, Eagles." Jerry Williams would be fired two weeks later; Leonard Tose would own the team for another 14 years, and the Eagles are still here.

10. Veterans Stadium: A, D, F; Franklin Field: B, E; Lincoln Financial Field: C.

 OVERTIME: *Uniform Number Question:* Tommy Thompson wore 10 before entering the service and switched to 11 when he got out of the service in 1945.

QUIZ ANSWERS !!!!

SECTION II

GLORY AND RIVALRIES

BACK-TO-BACK CHAMPIONSHIPS

1. The problem in the 1947 title game against the Cardinals was that the field was covered with ice. Before the game, the officials approved the cleats the Eagles were going to wear, but changed their ruling after the game started and the Eagle players were forced to change their shoes. On the slick field, Cardinal backs Elmer Angsman and Charley Trippi scored on long runs and returns of 44, 70, 75 and 70 yards to win the title 28-21. Eagles quarterback Tommy Thompson had a big day, completing 27 of 44 passes for 297 yards. Neale said afterwards, "We did everything but beat them" and complained, "We also had several new plays worked up for this game including cutbacks that we could not use."

2. A crew of 90 men, including many players from both teams, removed the heavy tarp, but the field was immediately recovered with snow. Because yard lines were invisible, first downs were awarded at the referee's discretion.

3. Bucko Kilroy recovered an Elmer Angsman fumble at the Cardinals' 17. Four runs later, one by each member of the backfield, the Eagles scored. Steve Van Buren got the TD on a five-yard run.

4. Because of the blizzard that did not let up during the game, Neale was afraid he would lose another title game because of flukey weather conditions.

5. Reserve end Leo Skladany, whose entire Eagle career consisted of the last three games of 1949, blocked a punt by Bob Waterfield and fell on the ball in the end zone.

6. A driving rainstorm that dumped 12 inches of precipitation on Los Angeles meant that only 22,000 fans turned out at the massive LA Coliseum, and the champion Eagles took home checks for only $1,090 each.

7. In both cases, the radio rights to the games had been sold, and he did not want to take a chance in messing that up with a time change when the NFL was really a second-rate league.

8. Van Buren gained 196 yards on 31 carries. No one ever gained more in an NFL championship. Timmy Smith of the Redskins gained 204 yards in the 1988 Super Bowl, but he was noted as having broken Marcus Allen's Super Bowl record of 191 yards since Super Bowls are considered a separate category than pre-Super Bowl championships. Keith Lincoln gained 206 yards on 13 carries in the 1963 AFL championship game.

9. All-Pro tackle Al Wistert, who often exhorted his teammates with pregame pep talks at Greasy Neale's behest.

10. No other professional football team has ever won consecutive shutout championships.

OVERTIME: *Uniform Number Question:* Rick Arrington, from Tulsa, who completed less than 50% of his passes from 1970 to 1972 and who threw three TDs and nine interceptions in that time. He is better known as the father of sexy contemporary sportscaster Jill Arrington.

QUIZ ANSWERS

1960

1. In a 41-24 loss to Cleveland at home, Norm Van Brocklin was booed for having three of his first six passes intercepted.

2. The Eagles managed to outlast Dallas 27-25 because defensive back Bobby Freeman blocked two extra-point attempts by Fred Cone. Dallas would not win a game all year.

3. After losing the opener, the Birds reeled off a team-record nine straight wins to clinch the Eastern crown. After losing to Pittsburgh, they finished the season 10-2 by beating Washington.

4. Five of the Eagles' victories were won in the final quarter in a comeback. Two of the comebacks were against the Giants and another thriller was against the Browns—their two biggest rivals for the title. The Browns rematch was won on Bobby Walston's 38-yard field goal with 10 seconds left after Van Brocklin led the Eagles back down the field from his own 10 in the final minute. The first Giants game featured Chuck Bednarik's legendary hit on Frank Gifford; in the second, they trailed 23-17 in the fourth quarter. Van Brocklin fired touchdown passes to backs Ted Dean and Billy Ray Barnes in the final period for a 31-23 victory.

5. The Eagles averaged only 3.2 yards per rush. The team leader was Clarence Peaks with 465 yards, but he was lost in the second half of the season and replaced by rookie Ted Dean.

6. The defense gave up 246 points in a 12-game season, 20.5 per game, seventh in a 13-team league.

7. Vince Lombardi's Packers had more yards (401 vs. 296), more first downs (22 vs. 13) and completed a higher percentage of passes (67% vs. 45%). They also had fewer points and lost 17-13.

8. Gauer noticed that the left side of the Packers' kick-return unit was slower than the right and designed a left return for the Birds in the fourth quarter. Ted Dean took the kick 58

yards to Green Bay's 38 to set up the winning drive.

9. Rookie Ted Dean scored on a five-yard sweep, which was ironic since that was the Packers' bread-and-butter play.

10. Defensive tackle Jess Richardson's seven-month-old baby died in his crib the week before the game, but the Philadelphia native played anyway.

OVERTIME: *Uniform Number Question:* Princeton's Bob Holly, a quarterback who never threw a pass for the Eagles. Jeff Kemp and Jay Fiedler both went to Dartmouth.

QUIZ ANSWERS 13
1980 SEASON: SUPER BOWL XV

1. The Eagles beat the Raiders 10-7 in late November in a very tough, bruising battle in which both touchdowns were scored in the final period. Ultimately, the Raiders were the first wild card team to get to the Super Bowl and win it.

2. While Carmichael was healthy, the other starting wide out, Charlie Smith, was playing with a broken jaw and third wide receiver Scott Fitzkee was out with a broken foot. In addition, tight end Keith Krepfle had shoulder problems and had missed three midseason games due to arthroscopic knee surgery. And Wilbert Montgomery, the team's leading rusher and receiver, had been banged up all season.

3. On a first-down play on the third play of the game, Jaws tried his first pass to tight end John Spagnola, but Rod Martin jumped in front of it and returned it to the Eagles' 30. Seven plays later, Jim Plunkett hit Cliff Branch with a two-yard scoring pass.

4. The Eagle pass rush smoked out the 33-year-old Plunkett later in the first quarter, but he spotted Kenny King on the sideline and lofted a pass just over the outstretched fingertips of cornerback Herman Edwards. King went 80 yards for the score to lead 14-0.

5. Franklin's attempt was smothered by 6'7" Raider linebacker Ted Hendricks. Blocking kicks was a particular specialty of the Hall of Famer whom the Eagles could have drafted instead of Leroy Keyes 12 years before.

6. Rod Martin nabbed his second interception, and it led to a Raider field goal to make the score 24-3.

7. Keith Krepfle, banged up but unrelenting, hauled in an eight-yard TD pass.

8. Jaws was trying to hit Wilbert Montgomery, who caught six passes for 91 yards that day. Martin's third pick led to another Oakland field goal to make the final score 27-10.

9. The Eagles fell behind so quickly that they could only gain 69 yards on the ground versus 117 by the Raiders.

10. Jaworski threw for more yards (290 vs. 261), but Plunkett's three touchdowns and one pick compared to Jaws' one touchdown and three picks made him the MVP.

 OVERTIME: *Uniform Number Question:* Fast and skinny Chuck Hughes from Texas Western wore 13 as a special teams player and receiver and caught six passes for Philadelphia from 1967 to 1969. In his second year in Detroit, he had a heart attack on the field against the Bears and died on October 24, 1971. Detroit retired his Lions number 85.

QUIZ ANSWERS 14

2004 SEASON: SUPER BOWL XXXIX

1. Both Jaworski and McNabb threw three interceptions in a losing effort despite throwing for more yardage than the winning quarterback.

2. Four-year flop Freddie Mitchell had the biggest game of his Eagle career by scoring twice against the Vikings, once by catching a TD pass and once by catching an L.J. Smith fumble in midair in the end zone.

3. Longtime Eagle tight end Chad Lewis caught two TD passes against the Falcons to help propel Philadelphia into the Super Bowl at last, but broke his foot in the process. Lewis' disappointment meant joy for his friend Jeff Thomason. The former Eagle tight end signed off a construction site to replace him.

4. While Owens caught nine passes for 122 yards, Deion Branch of the Patriots caught 11 for 133 and was named MVP.

5. L.J. Smith from six yards in the second quarter, Brian Westbrook from 10 yards in the third quarter and Greg Lewis from 30 yards in the fourth quarter.

6. The Eagles took a leisurely 3:48 to drive 79 yards in 13 plays and score on Greg Lewis'

30-yard TD catch with 1:52 remaining. To put it another way, the Eagles took 12 plays to move 49 yards. If the Patriot safety hadn't been in the wrong coverage, who knows how long it would have taken the Eagles to go those last 30 yards.

7. Patriot tight end Christian Fauria recovered the badly conceived, ill-fated onside kick.

8. After Josh Miller's 32-yard punt the Eagles took over on their own 4 with 46 seconds to play. If they hadn't tried the onside kick, they would probably have gotten the ball 25 to 30 yards further upfield.

9. Rather than throwing the ball upfield or even out of bounds, McNabb threw it back to the middle of the field deep in his own territory. Rather than deliberately dropping it, Westbrook caught it and was quickly tackled. By the time the Eagles regrouped and snapped the ball again, 30 seconds had ticked away.

10. Safety Rodney Harrison's second interception ended the game.

 OVERTIME: *Uniform Number Question:* Jeff Wilkins wore 14 for the Eagles in 1994. He also wore it in St. Louis when he kicked for Vermeil's Rams in the Super Bowl.

QUIZ ANSWERS

THE EAGLES IN THE PLAYOFFS

1. Everyone remembers the thrilling victory of the "Miracle of the Meadowlands" when the Eagles scored on an improbable fumble recovery in the closing seconds, but there was a poison pill in the win. In the second quarter the Eagles' mediocre kicker Nick Mike-Mayer lined up to attempt a field goal when due to a bad snap he ended up with the ball. He tried to throw a pass, but was injured instead. Inexplicably, Dick Vermeil elected to use his punter Mike Michel as his placekicker for the remaining four games. Even after watching Michel miss three of 12 extra-point attempts and not even try a single field goal in those games, Vermeil stayed with Michel for the very short playoff run.

2. We all remember how dominant the Eagles were that day, rushing for 254 yards, 194 by Wilbert. However, the score was tied 7-7 at the half. The second half could have gone either way, but the Eagle defense forced two third-quarter fumbles that led to points, and the ground attack held the ball for 12 minutes in the fourth quarter.

3. Return man Wally Henry fumbled a punt and a kickoff in the first quarter that led to the Giants leading 20-0 after one period. They held on for a 27-20 defeat of Philadelphia.

4. Down 7-0 in the first quarter, the Eagles got the ball deep in Bear territory on a Seth Joyner interception. Cunningham threw a nine-yard touchdown pass to Cris Carter, but it was nullified by a motion penalty on Anthony Toney. On the very next play, a 14-yard touchdown toss to Mike Quick was nullified by a holding penalty again on Toney, and the Eagles settled for a field goal. Later in the first quarter, Cunningham lost another TD pass when normally reliable Keith Jackson dropped a pass in the end zone. And the fog rolled in.

5. In the 1992 showdown between two clubs unable to win a playoff game, the Eagles fell behind the Saints early, but rolled in the second half. The scoring was closed out with a safety by Reggie White and an interception return by Eric Allen. Buddy's Boys won 36-20, but their coach was Rich Kotite.

6. Ray Rhodes' first playoff game was a shocker. The Eagle defense that featured a five-defensive-back alignment using safety Mike Zordich as a linebacker confused Lion quarterbacks Scott Mitchell and Don Majkowski so much that the Eagles garnered six interceptions and a fumble recovery that they converted into 34 points. Willie Thomas and Barry Wilburn returned picks for scores.

7. Twice in the first half, Detmer drove the Eagles inside the 49ers' 10 yard line; twice Ty ended those drives by throwing interceptions, and the Eagles never scored in a 14-0 loss.

8. In 2000, the Giants beat the Eagles without scoring an offensive touchdown. They scored on a kickoff return and on a spectacular interception and 32-yard return for a TD by Jason Sehorn. In 2001, the Eagles' last drive against the Rams was ended by Aeneas Williams' interception. The following year, Ronde Barber of the Bucs returned his interception 92 yards for the clinching fourth-quarter touchdown.

9. Mitchell's 28-yard miracle reception to the Packers' 46 didn't even get them into field goal range, but it demoralized Green Bay. The Eagles tied the game on a field goal, and won it in overtime after Brett Favre threw a pop-fly interception to Brian Dawkins to set up the winning three-pointer.

10. Pinkston caught 0 (after grabbing seven the week before), Thrash caught one for nine yards, while trash-talking Panther corner Ricky Manning, Jr. came away with three McNabb passes.

OVERTIME: *Uniform Number Question:* Lafayette "Reb" Russell wore 15 as an Eagle in their first year. 1933 was the former Northwestern All-American fullback's only season in the NFL, and he split it between the Giants and Eagles. He had had a couple of bit movie parts before joining the Eagles. However, after leaving, he starred in nine B Westerns with titles like *The Man from Hell, Cheyenne Tornado* and *Blazing Guns*. He also toured with the circus.

QUIZ ANSWERS 16

RIVALS: THE COWBOYS

1. In the next to last game of the 1967 season on December 10th, the Eagles met the Cowboys in Dallas. Early on, Philadelphia linebacker Mike Morgan hit quarterback Don Meredith late, broke his nose, and knocked him out of the game. The game then got out of hand; Norm Snead was sacked seven times and threw three interceptions in a 38-17 loss. Tom Woodeshick had his eye gouged, and Tim Brown had his face crushed on an incomplete pass by a Lee Roy Jordan cheap-shot elbow to the face. Tim suffered a concussion, a broken jaw and lost several teeth in his last game for the Eagles while Jordan received only a 15-yard penalty.

2. A second-round pick from Southern University, Ray Jones gave up TD passes of 86 and 56 yards to Lance Rentzel and 40 yards to Bob Hayes in a 21-17 Eagle loss. Ray was fast, but only lasted one year in Philly and parts of three others in San Diego and New Orleans.

3. In 1980, an out-of-bounds Carmichael was hit high by the Cowboys' Dennis Thurman in a cheap shot and knocked flat. Carmichael suffered back spasms and couldn't continue. Ironically, four years later, Harold caught his last pass as a Cowboy teammate of Thurman's.

4. In the 1987 players' strike, some of the Cowboys' stars crossed the picket line and played in the replacement games. Buddy Ryan encouraged his team to stick together on the picket line and resented Tom Landry's use of his stars to run up the score against the hapless Eagle replacements. When the real players returned, the first Eagle opponent was Dallas. With the Eagles handily beating Dallas 30-20 with seconds remaining, Buddy ordered Randall Cunningham to fake a kneel-down and throw a pass into the end zone for Mike Quick that drew an interference flag. Keith Byars then scored a touchdown to show up Landry and Dallas.

5. Clyde Simmons led the charge with a team record 4.5 sacks that day. The previous year, Simmons had dislocated Aikman's shoulder on a sack. Hugh Douglass later also recorded 4.5 sacks in a game.

6. Safety Tim Hauck nearly paralyzed Irvin in the incident recalled for the boorishness of fans cheering when the obnoxious Irvin was left motionless on the field.

7. The Eagles won the first match between the two in 1967, but from the Timmy Brown game through 1978, Dallas won 21 of 23 games; 15 of those Dallas wins were by double-digit margins.

8. The field goal measured 59 yards right before halftime, boosting the Eagles' lead to 17-7 in a game they would win 31-21. That snapped a nine-game Cowboy winning streak over Philadelphia.

9. Only one time before Reid had the Eagles scored 40 points against Dallas—in the second game of the series on October 22, 1961, Philadelphia pounded the Cowboys 43-7. By contrast, the Cowboys have scored 40 or more points against the Eagles six times. They did so four times in the 1960s, once in 1971, and the last time was the 1987 replacement-players game noted above in question 4.

10. At the end of a close game against the Cowboys with Dallas poised to score a winning touchdown, middle linebacker James Willis clinched the Eagle win by intercepting a Troy Aikman pass four yards deep in the end zone. At the Eagles' 10, Willis lateraled the ball to Vincent, and Troy took it the remaining 90 yards for the score in the Birds' 31-21 win.

 OVERTIME: *Uniform Number Question:* Quarterback Jeff Kemp wore 16 as an Eagle. His father Jack quarterbacked the Chargers and Bills before becoming a congressman, HUD secretary and vice presidential candidate.

QUIZ ANSWERS 17
RIVALS: THE GIANTS

1. By the end of the season, the inaugural Eagles had advanced from awful to mediocre and only lost the rematch 20-14 to finish at 3-5-2.

2. Greasy Neale, who coached against one of his closest friends in Giant coach Steve Owen. Neale went 10-9-1 against his old friend and personal rival. Owen helped Neale

with the draft in his early years, and Neale was responsible for sending Allie Sherman to New York to teach the Giants the T-Formation in the late 1940s. Owen finished his career as a defensive coach for the Eagles under Hugh Devore.

3. Charlie Conerly was so beaten up that his backup Fred Benners was inserted to take some of the beating the Eagles were doling out that day. The Eagles won 14-10. Some reports say that the Giants' QBs were sacked only 14 times, eight by Willey and six by Pete Pihos.

4. McDonald caught passes good for 237 yards against New York on December 10, 1961, but the Giants won 28-24 and clinched the divisional title.

5. Inconsistent Bobby Thomason had a big day on November 8, 1953 in a 30-7 win by throwing for 437 yards.

6. George Shaw was the quarterback who threw the pass and Chuck Weber was the middle linebacker who recovered the ball, ending the game and prompting Bednarik's celebration caught so well in the famous photograph.

7. Pisarcik was trying to get the ball into reliable Larry Csonka's hands. Giants offensive coordinator Bob Gibson was fired the next day for calling a running play rather than a kneel-down.

8. Luckily for Zendejas, Clyde Simmons grabbed the bouncing ball and chugged into the end zone with the winning points.

9. The Eagles gave a sixth-round pick for line coach Jerry Wampfler in 1978. Five years later, friction between Wampfler and center Guy Morris ended with both of them gone from Philadelphia.

10. Punt Returns: 87 yards, November 22, 1992, Vai Sikahema (punctuated by his punching out the goal post afterward); 84 yards, October 19, 2003, Brian Westbrook (with 1:30 to go, this return won the game and saved the season for Philadelphia); 81 yards, October 4, 1959, Tommy McDonald. TD Passes: 93 yards, September 4, 1994, Randall Cunningham to Herschel Walker; 92 yards, September 22, 1968, King Hill to Ben Hawkins; 91 yards, October 5, 1958, Norm Van Brocklin to Tommy McDonald. Tommy McDonald is the common denominator here, having scored on both a touchdown pass and punt return.

 OVERTIME: *Uniform Number Question:* Joe Carter, who twice led the team in receptions and led the NFL in yards per catch with 23.6 in 1935.

RIVALS: THE REDSKINS

1. On October 27, 1946, the Eagles fell behind 24-0 to the Redskins at halftime in Washington. In the second half, Tommy Thompson threw three TD passes, the last one 30 yards to Jack Ferrante with 90 seconds left in the game, and led the Birds to four second-half touchdowns for a 28-24 Eagles victory.

2. On November 1, 1959, the Redskins had a first and goal at the Eagles' 3 in the closing minute, trailing by a touchdown. A first-down run took them to the 1. Then, Washington fullback Don Bosseler was thwarted on three straight-line plunges from that point and the game ended on the Eagles' goal-line stand.

3. Fiery, vocal corner Ben Scotti, who regularly trash-talked Tommy McDonald, was beaten badly. For some reason, the Eagles saw fit to acquire Scotti the following season and that would lead to big problems in 1963 (see quiz #48).

4. Lud Wray was hired by George Marshall to coach the Boston Braves in 1932 and then replaced by real American Indian Lone Star Dietz in 1933. That year, Wray partnered with his old friend Bert Bell from the University of Pennsylvania to invest in the new Eagles franchise and become its first coach.

5. The two teams were not scheduled to meet in the Eagles' first year. The Boston Redskins beat the Eagles 6-0 on October 21, 1934; the Eagles took the rematch 7-6 in November.

6. The Redskins spent most of the day running the ball and built a 13-0 lead behind Sammy Baugh, the old TCU teammate of 5'7", 150-pound Davey O'Brien. O'Brien was passing the ball on almost every down, and he would complete a league record 33 of 60 passes for 316 yards that day. However, Philadelphia did not score until O'Brien completed a 13-yard touchdown to Frank Emmons in the fourth quarter. The Eagles got the ball back at their own 31 late and drove to the Redskins' 22 as time ran out but lost 13-7.

7. In a 45-42 Eagle victory on September 28, 1947, the big star was rookie end Pete Pihos who caught five passes for 89 yards and two scores. He just missed a third score by being brought down from behind at the goal line. It was an auspicious start for a Hall of Fame career.

8. Burk threw five more in the rematch to give him 12 against the Redskins that year and 11 against the rest of the league. Actually the 23 touchdowns were a personal record that he would never again approach. Burk, who had been obtained in a trade with Washington for Jack Dwyer, was an NFL official for many years after he retired as a player.

9. From 1954 to 1958, Kuharich's Redskins were 26-32-2, a .450 percentage, with one winning season; from 1964 to 1968, Kuharich's Eagles were 28-41-1, a .407 percentage, with

one winning season. Under Joe, Washington went 6-4 against Philadelphia, while the Eagles under Joe went 3-6-1 against the Redskins. Washington got the better part of this no matter how you slice it besides ending up with Sonny Jurgensen.

10. Defensive end N.D. Kalu, who went from the Eagles to the Redskins and then back to the Eagles, returned an interception of a Patrick Ramsey pass 15 yards for the winning touchdown in the third game the Eagles played at brand-new Lincoln Financial Field in 2003.

 OVERTIME: *Uniform Number Question:* Chris Boniol had made 87% of his field goals in three years in Dallas, but could only manage 69% accuracy in two years in Philadelphia.

QUIZ ANSWERS !!!!

SECTION III
PLAYERS AND POSITIONS

QUIZ ANSWERS 19

CHUCK BEDNARIK

1. True. After scoring on one of the 13 interceptions, Chuck was so excited that he fired the ball into the stands and drew a penalty.

2. True on all accounts. Bednarik also finished third in the vote for the Heisman as a senior. Chuck was probably the best player Penn ever had.

3. False. The champion Eagles won the lottery for the new bonus first pick of the draft and chose Bednarik. They then outbid the All-America Conference Brooklyn Dodgers to sign him, but he did not start immediately and complained to coach Greasy Neale about it. Neale worked Chuck into a rotation with center Vic Lindskog and linebacker Alex Wojciechowicz, two aging veterans that year.

4. False. The Eagles didn't even have a middle linebacker until halfway through Bednarik's career. They employed five defensive linemen and two outside linebackers. Bednarik did not move to the middle until halfway through the 1961 season.

5. False. Bednarik had played some at center in his first few years in Philadelphia but didn't move to the position full time until 1958, his tenth year. He was a good center, but a great linebacker. He spent his last two seasons back at linebacker.

6. True. Chuck announced his retirement before the end of the season and was given a "Day" before the final game against the Browns in 1959. However, his wife had their fifth child that spring, and he figured he could use the money, so he returned for the 1960 season.

7. False. Concrete Charlie had knocked the ball out of Mel Triplett's arms earlier in the fourth quarter, and Jimmy Carr grabbed the ball in midair and ran it in for the go-ahead score.

8. False. Chuck played both ways for parts of four games in 1960 due to injuries. He also played all the way in the championship game against the Packers.

9. False. Bednarik did make the final tackle of the NFL title game. However, safety Bobby Jackson had hold of Taylor's legs while Bednarik hit him high as was his style. Furthermore, when Taylor went down, only one to two seconds were left on the clock (there were nine seconds left when the play started at the 22), so there was no need to pin him.

10. True. Chuck wanted the Eagles to buy the extra warehouse copies of his 25-year-old autobiography and give them to the players. The Eagles said that would be considered compensation, and they couldn't do it. No compromise was worked out, and Chuck openly rooted against the Birds in Super Bowl XIX.

OVERTIME: *Uniform Number Question:* Bootin' Ben Agajanian, who lost his toes in a work accident, briefly appeared with the Eagles in 1945 wearing 89. Some 26 years later, Tom Dempsey, who was born with a deformed right arm and foot, wore 19 for the Eagles as their regular kicker for four years.

QUIZ ANSWERS 20
STEVE VAN BUREN

1. Steve Van Buren was born in Honduras to an American father and a Honduran mother. He grew up with his grandparents in Louisiana.

2. Steve weighed only 135 pounds as a high school junior. When he was cut from the team, he dropped out of school and worked in a steel mill for two years, building up his body. Thirty pounds stronger, he returned to school.

3. As a sophomore and junior, Van Buren blocked for star runner Alvin Dark, who gained greater fame as a baseball shortstop and manager. Finally as a senior, Steve got a chance to carry the ball and set a new Southeastern Conference rushing record that year.

4. Steve ran for a record 160 yards in the 1944 Orange Bowl. Five years later, he set the rushing record for an NFL title game with 196 against the Rams in the rain and mud.

5. Van Buren had vision problems in one eye and was given 4-F status by the selective service. The Eagles grabbed him in the first round despite never having seen him play on the basis of a personal recommendation made by LSU coach Bernie Moore to Greasy Neale.

6. Although his vision problems kept him from playing too much defense and from catching many passes on offense, Steve had a career-high five picks as a rookie.

7. Timmy Brown returned seven kicks for touchdowns in his years in Philadelphia; Van Buren is second on the team with five scoring returns—three on kickoffs and two on punts.

8. Van Buren led the league with 108 points on a record 18 touchdowns that year. That record was first tied by Jim Brown in 1958 and exceeded by Jim Taylor with 19 in 1962. Van Buren led the NFL in rushing touchdowns four times in his eight-year career.

9. Van Buren was the second NFL back to gain over 1,000 yards rushing and was the first to do it twice. Beattie Feathers of the Bears was the first to be credited with 1,000 yards rushing in a season, but some question the validity of that mark. Van Buren led the NFL in rushing four times in his eight-year career.

10. Both Neale and his assistant had played pro football with the legendary Hall of Famer Jim Thorpe and compared Steve's power to Thorpe's. Neale also compared Van Buren's elusiveness to Hall of Famer Red Grange. Van Buren's NFL record 5,860 yards was first topped by the 49ers Hall of Famer Joe "The Jet" Perry in 1958.

 OVERTIME: *Uniform Number Question:* Leroy Keyes was a two-way star for Purdue and the runner-up for the Heisman Trophy in 1968 after finishing third as a junior. As a pro, though, he was a flop as a runner and was no better than mediocre as a defensive back. At least he didn't kill anyone.

QUIZ ANSWERS 21

NORM VAN BROCKLIN

1. Pete Rozelle was a failure as GM, but two years later he would take over as NFL commissioner and become perhaps the most successful sports commissioner ever.

2. Bell indicated that the Eagle coach Buck Shaw only wanted to coach for a couple of years and retire. Bell promised the Eagle coaching job to Van Brocklin once Shaw stepped down.

3. Van Brocklin worked hard with second-year halfback Tommy McDonald, helping to turn him into the best deep threat in the league. He also saw great potential in Pete Retzlaff, who had been cut by the Lions and tried by the Eagles at fullback, end, defensive back and on special teams. Van Brocklin spent hours throwing passes to the two of them and likened Retzlaff's route-running to that of Ram Hall of Famer Elroy Hirsch.

4. Van Brocklin was the team's punter and averaged 43.1 yards in 1960.

5. O'Donoghue's. Aside from Pete Retzlaff who didn't drink, Chuck Bednarik and the three black players on the team (Timmy Brown, Ted Dean and Clarence Peaks) who didn't feel comfortable in the place, the rest of the team would show up there on the Monday after a game. The 1960 Eagles forged a strong brotherhood in their Monday sessions.

6. In the third quarter the Eagles trailed the Browns 22-7, but Van Brocklin led the team to three touchdowns, including scoring passes to Tommy McDonald and Billy Ray Barnes, to take a 28-22 lead. Bobby Mitchell's TD reception put the Browns back on top, but Van Brocklin drove the Birds from their own 10 to Cleveland's 31 in the final minute. With 10 seconds left, Bobby Walston's 38-yard field goal gave the Eagles a 31-29 victory. Still, 38

yards was actually beyond the limit for the aging Walston's leg. Of greatest importance, the team began to believe something special was happening.

7. Pistol Pete Retzlaff's 41-yard reception in the second quarter led to a 15-yard field goal by Bobby Walston.

8. Coach Buck Shaw in the locker room after the game.

9. Van Brocklin became the first coach of the expansion Minnesota Vikings.

10. In six years in Minnesota and seven in Atlanta, Van Brocklin's teams had three winning seasons. The caustic sarcasm of Van Brocklin's tongue was easier to take when he was a player and could back up his perfectionist tendencies on the field.

> **OVERTIME:** *Uniform Number Question:* Undersized safety Joe Scarpati wore 21 as the Eagles' defensive MVP in 1966 and for six other years in town. He also played in New Orleans where he was the holder for future Eagle Tom Dempsey's record 63-yard field goal.

QUIZ ANSWERS
TOMMY McDONALD

1. Tommy McDonald played under Bud Wilkinson at the University of Oklahoma when the Sooners were setting a record by winning 47 straight games. In his three years on the varsity, Oklahoma went 30-0. The Eagles were a big change for him as they were 4-8 in 1957 and 2-9-1 in 1958.

2. McDonald won the Maxwell Award and finished third for the Heisman just as Chuck Bednarik did eight years before him. Despite the notoriety, he was only a third-round pick of the Eagles.

3. Tommy primarily came to accept his Maxwell Award and to negotiate his contract as a sidelight. After signing for $12,000, Tommy did some sightseeing in town before stopping at a travel agency to buy a return plane ticket. The next thing he knew, he was being arrested because of his close resemblance to the Lonely Hearts Bandit, who was then notorious for robbing small businesses in the city and tying up the female employees. When tiny Tommy tried to tell the police that he was in town to sign a contract to play for the Eagles, the cops thought that was a joke. Finally, he convinced them to check with Eagles GM Vince McNally, and the matter was cleared up.

4. While Philadelphia was winning just two of its first eight games, McDonald was used primarily as a return man and a backup halfback on offense. Finally, in the ninth game against the Redskins, Tommy got his chance to start at flanker due to assistant coach Charlie Gauer's advocacy, and he caught two touchdown passes from fellow rookie Sonny Jurgensen in an Eagle victory. The first score went for 61 yards with McDonald outleaping the defender for the ball. In the last four games of the season, fledgling receiver McDonald caught nine passes for three touchdowns.

5. McDonald claims to be the last NFL player to perform without a face mask, although there are pictures of him wearing a single-bar face mask.

6. Tommy was the Eagle touchdown king. McDonald caught a touchdown every 4.35 catches; Cris Carter caught one every 4.68 catches; Jack Ferrante caught one every 5.45 catches; Mike Quick caught one every 5.95 catches; Harold Carmichael caught one every 7.45 catches.

7. Owens caught 14 touchdowns in 14 games in 2004. McDonald set the record of 13 touchdowns in a 12-game season in 1960 and equaled it the following year in a 14-game season. McDonald broke the prior record of 11 touchdowns attained by Pete Pihos in 1948 and Bobby Walston in 1954, both 12-game seasons.

8. McDonald led the league in touchdowns in 1958 with nine and in 1961 with the aforementioned 13. In 1960, Tommy's 13 was topped by the Cardinals' Sonny Randle with 15. Tommy also led the NFL in receiving yards with 1,144 in 1961.

9. When Tommy scored a touchdown, he liked to celebrate. Often, he took off toward a teammate and jumped into his arms or on his back. Tommy was a physical player in his own way.

10. The Bee Gees' disco hit "Staying Alive." The sight of a 62-year-old man disco-dancing at his Hall of Fame induction was something that no one who was there will ever forget.

 OVERTIME: *Uniform Number Question:* Now a local sportscaster, Vai Sikahema celebrated his 87-yard punt return touchdown in Tommy McDonald fashion by treating the goal post like a speed bag. This 1992 punt return TD was the longest in team history.

HAROLD CARMICHAEL AND WILBERT MONTGOMERY

1. Boyd Dowler, who was a 6'5" wide receiver for Vince Lombardi's Packers before becoming the passing game coach under Mike McCormack, suggested trying Carmichael out on the wing.

2. Harold led the NFL in 1973 with 67 catches and 1,116 yards and helped the Eagles double their point total from the previous year. Both figures were personal bests that he never exceeded.

3. Abramowicz caught a pass in an NFL-best 105 consecutive games. Harold tied the record against the Bengals on October 28th and broke it on November 4th. Carmichael ran the streak to 127 before it ended in the last game of the 1980 season against the Cowboys. Carmichael's 127-game streak was broken by Steve Largent in 1986, and Largent pushed the mark up to 177 games before retiring. Art Monk broke that in 1994 and extended the record to 183 before quitting. Jerry Rice passed Monk in 1998 and was not shut out until 2004 as a Raider after 274 games.

4. The Eagles presented Harold with a trophy over 23 feet tall to commemorate the occasion and gave his wife a bouquet of 106 roses. Carmichael donated the trophy to the Hall of Fame, but his wife kept the roses.

5. At the end of the 1980 season, Carmichael passed Pete Retzlaff's 452 catches to become the all-time leading Eagle receiver. He finished with 589 catches for 8,978 yards and 79 touchdowns as an Eagle.

6. Wilbert Montgomery's brother Cleo was a kick returner who played six years for the Bengals, Browns and Raiders, while his brother Tyrone was a running back who played two years for the Raiders. Both of the two brothers scored one touchdown in the NFL; Wilbert scored 58.

7. After transferring from Jackson State to Abilene Christian, Wilbert set a college record by scoring 37 touchdowns as a freshman tailback. He would go on to rush for over 3,000 yards and score 76 touchdowns in his college career. In addition, he was a sprinter on the track team, running the 100 in 9.6 and the 220 in 20.8.

8. In 1975, the Eagles traded journeyman guard Mark Nordquist to the Bears for a ninth-round pick in 1976 that they used to select fullback Mike Hogan and a sixth-round pick in 1977 that they used to grab Montgomery. He went so low because scouts questioned his size and his susceptibility to injury.

9. Wilbert was the first Eagle since Steve Van Buren in 1949 to gain over 1,000 yards on the ground, a drought of 28 years. Since Montgomery left, Ernest Jackson, Herschel Walker, Ricky Watters and Duce Staley have all repeated the accomplishment.

10. Wilbert led the Eagles in rushing six times (the same as Steve Van Buren) and went over

1,000 three times. Ricky Watters and Duce Staley both duplicated Montgomery's hat trick of three seasons over 1,000, but only Wilbert has three seasons over 1,200 yards.

 OVERTIME: *Uniform Number Question:* Harry Jones, a running back from Arkansas, gained 85 yards in 44 carries over four injury-plagued seasons. In their draft slot, the Eagles could have selected Hall of Famers Willie Lanier or Lem Barney.

QUIZ ANSWERS 24
BILL BERGEY

1. Bill Bergey and Bill Clinton were both called "Bubba." Before Clinton was elected governor, Bergey was named Arkansas State's all-time greatest player and had his number 66 retired there.

2. Bergey was drafted by the second-year expansion Cincinnati Bengals in the second round of the 1969 draft. He was an immediate starter and made the AFL All-Star Game as a rookie.

3. In 1974, Bill signed a future contract with the Virginia Ambassadors of the brand-new World Football League for 1976 after the option year in his Bengal contract ran out. Paul Brown of the Bengals did not want a lame duck middle linebacker, so he traded his rights to the Eagles. Meanwhile, the WFL team moved to Florida and reneged on Bergey's bonus payments before they ever took the field, which freed Bill and made him an Eagle.

4. Mike McCormack, who had played under Paul Brown but emulated George Allen, was the coach and GM of the Eagles. He gave up two number one picks (who would turn out to be Wilson Whitley and Ross Browner) and a number two (who would be Ray Griffin). That was a lot to give up, but it is the one McCormack trade that could be fully justified because Bergey was that good.

5. The Bergey Bunch of Eagle linebackers were Tom Ehlers, Frank LeMaster, John Bunting, Kevin Reilly, Jim Opperman, Dean Halverson and Bergey himself.

6. Bergey led the team in tackles six times in seven years. The only year he missed was 1979 when he tore up his knee in the third game of the year.

7. Bill was named All-Pro each year from 1974 to 1978 and went to four Pro Bowls as both a middle linebacker and an inside linebacker after the Eagles switched to a 3-4 defense in 1977.

8. Super Bowl XV against the Raiders. Bergey rehabbed hard after his 1979 injury to return to the field in 1980, but he was no longer the force he had been. He had lost his speed and was in pain, but persevered through the season on guts and experience.

9. Like Tommy Brookshier before him, Bergey didn't want to walk away from the game. He spent the 1981 season on injured reserve, hoping he would be able to return the following year. However, when his knee did not come around, he retired immediately after the 1981 season.

10. Jake and Josh made their names in the National Lacrosse League. Both played for the Philadelphia Wings.

 OVERTIME: *Uniform Number Question:* George Taliaferro started out with the Los Angeles Dons in the All-America Conference. Later he played some quarterback with the New York Yanks, Dallas Texans and Baltimore Colts in the NFL before winding up his career as a defensive back in Philadelphia in 1954.

QUIZ ANSWERS

RON JAWORSKI

1. Jaworski was drafted by the Rams in the second round of the 1973 draft. Drafted ahead of him were Bert Jones in the first round and Gary Huff in the second. After him came Gary Keithley in the second and Joe Ferguson and Dan Fouts in the third.

2. Jaws spent three years mostly as a backup in Los Angeles, although he started and won a playoff game for them against the Cardinals in 1975. In 1977, Dick Vermeil sent the rights to talented but difficult tight end Charles Young to the Rams for Jaworski. It worked out well for both sides.

3. 344 times including 88 times in his first two seasons in Philadelphia.

4. 32, and Jaws kept on going. Troy Aikman and Steve Young had much greater problems from much fewer concussions.

5. Favre's record is 221 consecutive starts through the 2005 season. He passed Jaworski's old record of 116 in 1999. Although Favre has thrown nearly 3,000 more passes in his 15-year career, he has only been sacked 16 more times than Jaws was, again through the 2005 season.

6. The Bert Bell Trophy for the NFL MVP. It was his best year by far—3,529 yards, 27 touchdowns, only 12 interceptions and a Super Bowl trip.

7. Three times each. Jaworski threw for 20 touchdowns in 1980, 1981 and 1983. Conversely, he threw at least 20 picks in 1977, 1981 and 1985.

8. Only one, fewest interceptions (six) in 1986. That was his last year in Philadelphia, and Jaws spent it suffering under Buddy Ryan's strange practice of pulling him on third and long situations to insert Randall Cunningham.

9. If you consider Jaworski at least partly Cunningham's backup in 1986, then you can add Miami's Dan Marino in 1988 and Kansas City's Steve DeBerg in 1989.

10. The Philadelphia Soul of the Arena League.

 OVERTIME: *Uniform Number Question:* "The Baron" Pete Retzlaff wore 25 when he first came to the Eagles in 1956. He switched to 44 in 1957 when Tommy McDonald arrived and claimed 25. And 44 is retired for Retzlaff.

QUIZ ANSWERS

REGGIE WHITE

1. The Eagles selected White in the USFL supplemental draft in 1984. He and Steve Young were the two Hall of Famers available in that draft.

2. Reggie recorded 13 sacks as an NFL rookie in 1985 with the Eagles. However, he had also played 18 games with the Memphis Showboats of the USFL in the spring and recorded 11.5 sacks there. So you could say he recorded 24.5 sacks in 1985.

3. Since Smiley Creswell was wearing 92, Reggie wore 91 when he sacked Phil Simms 2.5 times in his first game as an Eagle. The immortal Creswell moved on shortly after that and Reggie took 92.

4. In 1989 Reggie recorded "only" 11 sacks. In his eight years as an Eagle, Reggie totaled a team record 124 sacks, an average of 15.5 per year; in his six seasons as a Packer, he

totaled 68.5, an average of 11.5 per year. Norman Braman was correct that Green Bay got Reggie's declining years, but they also got a championship.

5. Reggie was the "Big Dawg" because he was the leader on any team of which he was a member; he was also called the "Minister of Defense" because of his religious leanings. The latter would also be the subtitle of the second of his three autobiographies, that one published in 1991.

6. Reggie recorded 21 sacks in 1987, the strike season when replacement players took the field for three games and a fourth game was wiped out. So White totaled 21 sacks in a 12-game season, 1.75 per game.

7. Reggie set another league record by being selected for 13 straight Pro Bowls, the first seven as an Eagle. He was also named Defensive Player of the Year four times: 1987, 1991, 1995 and 1998.

8. Three. Reggie first retired with a bad back after the Packers' second Super Bowl appearance in 1998; he had a record 176.5 sacks at the time. A week later, he rescinded his retirement notice and said he was feeling better. In the 1998 season, he attained his sack total, 16, since coming to Green Bay. However, most were from the first half of the year, and he was clearly running out of gas by the end of the season. At his second retirement, White had a record 192.5 sacks. A year later in 2000, he came back again with the Panthers, possibly because Bruce Smith was closing in on his career sack record. He managed a career-low 5.5 sacks in 2000 and retired for good with a record 198 sacks in 15 seasons. Three years later, Bruce Smith ended his 19-year career with a new record of 200 sacks.

9. White's was the lead name in a class action antitrust suit that several players filed against the NFL in 1992. The suit led to a collective bargaining agreement in 1993 that instituted free agency in pro football, and Reggie was the first star to take advantage of it by leaving the Eagles whose management had frustrated him for years.

10. On December 5, 2005, during the halftime ceremonies of a pathetic, rainy *Monday Night Football* trouncing by the Seahawks, the Eagles officially retired Reggie's number 92. The team was already behind 35-0 in what would end as a 42-0 loss to a Seattle team coached by Reggie's coach in Green Bay, Mike Holmgren. Since the Packers had already retired 92 for Reggie, he is the only NFL player to have his number retired by more than one team.

QUIZ ANSWERS 27

RANDALL CUNNINGHAM

1. Randall's big brother Sam starred for the USC Trojans before moving on to the New England Patriots. Some dime-store psychologists trace Cunningham's insecurities to the fact that both his parents died when Randall was young, and he was estranged from his revered older brother.

2. One of the biggest hits on the Cunningham highlight reel came in 1988 when Randall rolled right and found linebacker Carl Banks going for his legs. Cunningham broke his hurdling fall with his hand, popped up and threw a TD pass to tight end Jimmie Giles.

3. Another amazing play from the highlight reel came in 1990 against the Bills. Cunningham dropped back in his own end zone, eluded the charging Bruce Smith, dashed to his left and launched the ball 60 yards in the air where Fred Barnett leaped to snare it and race the rest of the way on a remarkable 95-yard touchdown pass play.

4. The longest punt was 91 yards and came against the Giants in 1989. Randall also uncorked an 80-yard punt against the Cowboys in 1994.

5. Randall threw for 407 yards, but had 0 touchdowns, three interceptions and only 12 points. In his defense, two TD passes were called back on penalties and another was dropped in the end zone.

6. Four seasons, from 1987 through 1990. In addition, Cunningham was second to Keith Byars by 37 yards in 1986. The pinnacle was 1990 when he gained 942 yards rushing and threw for over 3,400 yards—and that was his third straight year with over 3,000 yards passing. Then in 1991, Randall was injured in the opening game of the season. While he won Comeback Player of the Year in 1992, he was never the same player again.

7. Randall went into the masonry business in Nevada.

8. "Any questions, call my agent" was on a T-shirt Randall wore to his first training camp as a jheri-curled rookie. "Let me be me" was a slogan on a hat another year. "I'm still scrambling" was worn on a hat, too, but it also was the title of his 1993 autobiography.

9. The party was for Whitney Houston. This was before Bobby Brown.

10. Cunningham won the Bert Bell Trophy in 1988, 1990 and again in 1998 with the Vikings when his bombs to Randy Moss almost brought the 15-1 Vikings to the Super Bowl. With Randall, it was always "almost."

 OVERTIME: *Uniform Number Question:* Clyde "Smackover" Scott was an early contender for Steve Van Buren's successor, but the injury problems ended his career.

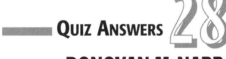

Quiz Answers

DONOVAN McNABB

1. McNabb was a reserve on the 1996 Final Four basketball team at Syracuse under Jim Boeheim.

2. Only Tim Couch. McNabb was the second player and quarterback picked that year. After him came Akili Smith at third, Daunte Culpepper at 11th and Cade McNown at 12th. Cade McNown was out of football in 2002; Akili Smith dropped out in 2003; Tim Couch flopped in 2004. Culpepper, like McNabb, had a terrific year in 2004 and an awful one both on and off the field in 2005.

3. John Reaves in 1972. Reaves never got much coaching and never developed as an NFL quarterback. He bounced from Philadelphia to Cincinnati to Minnesota to Houston and then out of the league. After finally achieving success in the USFL, Reaves briefly returned to the NFL as a replacement player with Tampa in 1987.

4. When the negotiations for McNabb's first pro contract in 1999 began to break down over the issue of voidable years, his agent Fletcher Smith gave a TV interview in which he suggested that the Eagles were reluctant to give McNabb a contract without voidable years because of his race. Smith was videotaped saying, "There's not much history with black quarterbacks, but you definitely don't want to see Tim Couch, Peyton Manning, Ryan Leaf, Kerry Collins get the kind of deals they got, and it was no issue. We'll pay

these guys. Why pull the plug now when for the past couple of years you've been consistently doing it for the white quarterbacks?" McNabb and Smith quickly backed away from those comments when they saw the public reaction.

5. Just once in 2000 with 629 yards, unlike the Eagles' earlier mobile quarterback Randall Cunningham, who led the team four times. While both had great running skill, Randall was forced to rely more on his legs due to having a weaker line, a worse running game and an inferior offensive scheme.

6. The previous best for an Eagle quarterback was four times under Ron Jaworski from 1978 to 1981. Tommy Thompson led the team to three straight championship games from 1947 to 1949.

7. During the first half, McNabb injured his ankle, but continued to hobble around and play the entire second half, tossing those four scores and leading the team to victory. The next day, it was revealed that he had a broken ankle and would miss the rest of the season. Under Koy Detmer and A.J. Feeley the Eagles rallied and won five of their last six games, and Donovan returned for the playoffs.

8. Only two: in 2000, when he ran for 629 yards, McNabb led the league with a 7.3 rushing average, and in 2002, he threw the fewest interceptions of any qualifying passer. The only Eagle quarterback ever to lead the NFL in passing was Tommy Thompson in 1948.

9. Donovan McNabb, 357 in 2004; Tommy Thompson, 297 in 1947; Ron Jaworski, 290 in 1980; and Norm Van Brocklin, 204 in 1960. Only Van Brocklin wound up a winner in these four games.

10. It was very strange how McNabb injected race into an already embarrassing situation. He first brought up a couple of white receivers in regard to Owens. "That's like me going out and saying, 'Hey, if we had Steve Largent. If we had Joe Jurevicius.' It was definitely a slap in the face to me. It was a slap in the face because, as deep as people want to go into it, it was black-on-black crime." Then, instead of seeing the real insult as that of being compared negatively to a formerly great quarterback who has slipped badly, he intimated that it would have been alright if Owens had compared him unfavorably to other black quarterbacks. "It's different to say, 'If we had Michael Vick or Daunte Culpepper or Steve McNair or Byron Leftwich,' but to go straight to Brett Favre, that kind of just slapped me in the face."

 OVERTIME: *Uniform Number Question:* Super Bill Bradley, who led the NFL in interceptions in 1971 and 1972, was related to noted five-star general Omar Bradley.

EAGLE QUARTERBACKS

1. In 1956, Bob Thomason completed 50% of his passes for four touchdowns and 21 interceptions and a quarterback rating of 40.7; in 1950, Tommy Thompson completed 40.7% of his passes for 11 touchdowns and 22 interceptions and a quarterback rating of 44.4; in 1951, Adrian Burk completed 42.2% of his passes for 14 touchdowns and 23 interceptions and a quarterback rating of 44.5; in 1998, Bobby Hoying completed 50.9% of his passes for 0 touchdowns and nine interceptions and a quarterback rating of 45.6.

2. While George Taliaferro had played quarterback for other NFL teams, he did not play the position for the Eagles. Fresh out of the World Football League, Johnnie Walton in 1976 became the first black quarterback to play for the Eagles.

3. Davey O'Brien, John Huarte and Ty Detmer won the Heisman. Jurgensen played in a running offense and barely threw the ball at Duke. John Reaves and Koy Detmer were stars in college, but did not win the Heisman.

4. All won the Davey O'Brien Award for best college quarterback except Donovan McNabb.

5. All won the Johnny Unitas Award for best college quarterback except Donovan McNabb.

6. Greg Barton threw one incomplete pass for the Detroit Lions in 1969, and that encouraged the Eagles to give up three high draft picks for him in 1971. To top off the embarrassment, Barton spurned the Eagles and signed with a Canadian team instead.

7. Bobby Thomason cost one number one and change, as did Norm Van Brocklin, King Hill and Mike Boryla. Roman Gabriel cost two number ones, a number three and Harold Jackson. Matt Cavanaugh only cost a number two and three, but that was still too much for him.

8. All played for the Rams before the Eagles, but Jeff Kemp made stops in San Francisco and Seattle before coming to Philadelphia.

9. All except Rodney Peete were named to at least one Pro Bowl. Boryla is the surprise because all the others were inconsistent, but had some good years. Boryla was invited after the first six choices bailed out. He still didn't deserve it, but played very well in leading the NFC to a fourth-quarter comeback victory in 1976.

10. Tommy Thompson threw 25 TDs in 1948. To put this into perspective, Thompson was only the third passer in league history to reach 25 touchdown passes. The first two were Hall of Famer Sid Luckman with 28 in 1943 and Hall of Famer Sammy Baugh with 25 in 1947. Thompson was among the top signal callers of his time.

OVERTIME: *Uniform Number Question:* Mark McMillian was a 5'7" cornerback who had a big heart and a bigger mouth.

QUIZ ANSWERS

EAGLE RUNNING BACKS

1. Thomas "Swede" Hanson from Temple University was the team's first star. He led the Eagles in rushing for their first four years and finished second in the NFL with 805 yards in 1934. In the Philly papers, Hanson was called the "Red Grange of the locals." He was 6'1" and 192 pounds—lean, lank, lantern-jawed and limber.

2. None of them ever reached 1,000 yards in a season. They could be called the "not quite" club. Tom "Silky" Sullivan came closest to 1,000 with 968 yards one year.

3. Earnest Jackson was a plodding runner who gained 1,028 yards on 286 carries, an average of only 3.6 yards per carry in 1985. Buddy Ryan was so desperate to unload Jackson when he took over as coach in 1986 that he simply cut him at the beginning of the season.

4. This is a question that can be interpreted in different ways. John Huzvar gained 349 yards in 1952. However, that was a 12-game season and his per game average was 29. In 1994, James Joseph led the Eagles with 440 yards in a 16-game season, an average of only 27.5 yards per game.

5. Two Eagles, Po James and Tom Sullivan, led the team in rushing yet only averaged 3.1 yards per carry. James gained 565 yards on 182 carries in 1972, an extended average of 3.10; Sullivan gained 760 yards on 244 carries in 1974, an extended average of 3.11. James did worse.

6. Fast scatback Bosh Pritchard gained 506 yards on 84 carries, an average of six yards per carry.

7. Those are all-purpose yards. Timmy Brown was a shifty runner, fast punt and kick returner and dangerous receiver for the Eagles in the 1960s. His main problems were staying healthy and avoiding fumbles.

8. Keith Byars caught 371 passes for the Eagles, not counting the year he spent as a tight end.

9. Ricky Watters gained over 1,000 yards once in San Francisco, three times in Philadelphia and three times in Seattle. He ended his career with 10,643 yards rushing and over 4,000 yards receiving.

10. Duce Staley went over 1,000 yards three times as an Eagle and was named offensive MVP each time. Although he has been injured most of his time in Pittsburgh, he still got a ring for the Steelers' Super Bowl XL win.

OVERTIME: *Uniform Number Question:* Alvin "Juggy" Haymond returned two kicks for scores in his one year in Philadelphia before being traded to the Rams for Jimmy Raye and Billy Guy Anderson, another bad trade for the Eagles.

QUIZ ANSWERS

EAGLE RECEIVERS

1. Joe Carter led the NFL in receiving average in 1935 with a mark of 23.6 yards per catch. He played for the Birds from 1933 to 1940 and caught his 100th pass in 1939. He caught 114 passes for 21 touchdowns as an Eagle.

2. Bill "Stinky" Hewitt was a perennial All-Pro for the Bears when Bert Bell obtained him in a trade in 1937. With the Eagles, he became the first NFL player named All-Pro from two different teams. He was particularly noted as a terror on defense and was the last Eagle to play without a helmet. He retired after the 1939 season but returned during the war in 1943, wearing a helmet for the first time.

3. Pete Pihos, the "Golden Greek," led the NFL in receptions from 1953 to 1955. He also led twice in yards and once in TD catches. He was named All-Pro eight times and selected for the first six Pro Bowls. He even made All-Pro in 1952 when he switched over to defense for one year.

4. Frank Budd from Villanova held the record for the 100-yard dash at 9.2 seconds, but flopped as a receiver for the Eagles in 1962, catching five passes for 130 yards and a touchdown. He spent one more season in Washington before disappearing from football. The track star who broke Budd's dash record at 9.1 seconds won an Olympic Gold Medal and became a star receiver for the Cowboys just a couple years later. His name was Bullet Bob Hayes.

5. Harold Jackson started with the Rams and came to the Eagles in a trade for Izzy Lang in 1969. He led the NFL in receiving yards in 1969 and 1972 and in catches in 1972 as well. In 1973, he was traded back to the Rams along with two number one picks and a number three for Roman Gabriel. He had several more years as a dangerous deep threat for

the Rams and Patriots before finishing his career with the Vikings and Seahawks.

6. Bobby Walston in 1951, Charles Young in 1973 and Keith Jackson in 1988 were all Rookie of the Year. Although he wasn't really a tight end as a rookie, Walston lasted 12 years in Philadelphia, caught 311 passes and is still the team's all-time leading scorer with 881 points. Young caught 197 balls in four years before being traded for Ron Jaworski. Jackson caught 242 passes in four years before going to Miami as a free agent.

7. The top two seasons for receptions in Eagle history were 88 by the 34-year-old Irving Fryar in 1996 and 86 by the 35-year-old Irving Fryar in 1997. Time and poor quarterbacking began to catch up to him the following year when he dropped to 48 catches in his final year in Philadelphia.

8. As a rookie, Mike Quick caught only 10 passes in the strike-shortened season of 1982. He blossomed in his second year, catching 69 passes for 13 touchdowns with an average gain of over 20 yards per catch. Over the next five years, Quick averaged 62 catches and 11 TDs per year before he began to suffer a series of knee and leg injuries that unfortunately shortened his career.

9. After graduating from the University of Minnesota, Bud Grant signed with the NBA's Minneapolis Lakers and played two years for the basketball champions before returning to football by signing with the Eagles, who had picked him first in the 1950 draft. He spent his rookie year on defense, switched with Pete Pihos in 1952 and caught 56 passes, the second leading total in the league. He also became the first Eagle to gain over 200 yards receiving in one game with 203 yards on 11 catches against the Texans that December. Grant then jumped to the CFL where he followed his playing career with a successful coaching one in both the CFL and NFL.

10. Andy Reid signed free agent Redskin tight end Jamie Asher to a $4.1 million contract in 1999. Asher broke his ankle on the sixth play from scrimmage and never played again.

 OVERTIME: *Uniform Number Question:* Irv Kupcinet played part of 1935 as a blocking back for the Eagles before quitting to go into journalism in his hometown of Chicago.

EAGLE OFFENSIVE LINEMEN

1. The Bears traded Santa Clara's Dick Bassi to the Eagles for the rights to Santa Clara center John Schiechl. Dick was an All-Pro guard in Philadelphia in 1940 before moving on to the 49ers after the war to play under Buck Shaw, his old Santa Clara coach.

2. Pro Bowl center Ken Farragut played for the Eagles from 1951 to 1954. He was a direct descendant of Admiral David Farragut, who was the Commander in Chief of the Union Navy during the Civil War. In attempting to take the mined Bay of Mobile, Alabama, Farragut had himself lashed to the rigging of his ship and ordered his fleet, "Damn the torpedoes, full speed ahead!" Most of the ships succeeded in getting through.

3. The Eagles had two Sons of Italy starting at guard in 1944. Enio Conti was born in Naples and graduated from Bucknell. He joined the Eagles from the Giants' Jersey City minor league team, but was forced to retire in 1945 due to high blood pressure. Bruno Banducci hailed from Tasignano, grew up in California and received a degree in engineering from Stanford. He moved on to the 49ers in 1946.

4. Bucko Kilroy, who played offense and defense at tackle and guard over his 13 years as an Eagle, wore 76 from 1943 to 1955; J.D. Smith was the best lineman for the 1960 champs and played as an Eagle from 1959 to 1963; Hall of Famer Bob "Boomer" Brown anchored the Eagle line from 1964 to 1968; Jerry Sisemore was a quiet, steady performer for Philadelphia from 1973 to 1984.

5. Stan Campbell started for the Lions when they won their final title in 1957, and started one more season in Detroit before future All-Pro John Gordy was drafted to replace him in 1959. He was traded to the Eagles and started for the 1960 champs. However, as with Detroit, Campbell lasted just one more year with Philadelphia after the championship. Neither the Lions nor the Eagles have won a championship since they let go of Campbell. Could Detroit and Philadelphia be suffering from the Campbell curse?

6. Holding penalties. Howell was obtained from the Giants for discontented guard Pete Case and showed talent but too much of a propensity for holding from 1965 to 1969.

7. College teammates Bob Suffridge and Burr West joined the Eagles together in 1941 from Tennessee and then went into the military. That year their Volunteer teammate, center Ray "Parson" Graves, came to Philadelphia and played from 1942 to 1943 before going into the service, too. Graves later had a Hall of Fame coaching career at Florida where he mentored Steve Spurrier. Suffridge came back for one more year as an Eagle in 1945.

8. Michigan retired 11 for the three Wistert brothers who wore the number as All-American tackles for the Wolverines. Francis played at Ann Arbor from 1931 to 1933, Albert from 1940 to 1942 and Alvin from 1947 to 1949. Albert was the Eagles' captain and a perennial All-Pro; he had his number 70 retired by the team in 1951 upon his retirement.

9. Otis Douglas played football at William & Mary in 1929-30. He signed on with the Eagles as a 35-year-old rookie tackle and part-time trainer in 1946 and stayed for four years. He later coached at the college level and in the CFL. The Cincinnati Reds brought Douglas in as a trainer in 1961, and they went to the World Series for the first time since 1919 when Eagle coach Greasy Neale was a Reds outfielder.

10. Walter "Piggy" Barnes got his start as an actor for local television while he played in Philadelphia. Piggy was the most successful of all Eagles who dabbled in acting. He appeared with Eastwood in *High Plains Drifter, Cahill: U.S. Marshall, Every Which Way But Loose* and *Bronco Billy*. Barnes retired from acting in the late 1980s and moved into the Motion Picture and Television Retirement Home where he died in 1998 at the age of 79.

OVERTIME: *Uniform Number Question:* Runner Herb Lusk was called the "Praying Tailback" as an Eagle from 1976 to 1978 because he was the first NFL player to crouch in prayer following a touchdown. When his Eagles career was over, he followed his father's example and became the pastor at the Greater Exodus Baptist Church on Broad Street. He has drawn attention for his support of President Bush in the current decade.

QUIZ ANSWERS 33
EAGLE DEFENDERS

1. Eric Allen, a second-round pick of Buddy Ryan's, intercepted 34 passes and returned five for touchdowns in seven seasons as an Eagle. His most memorable moment in Philadelphia was his twisting, turning 94-yard interception return for a touchdown against the Jets in 1993. After he left as a free agent, he accumulated another 20 picks for three more scores in six more years in New Orleans and Oakland.

2. Don "Blade" Burroughs, a 6'4", 180-pound free safety best known for his ball-hawking skills. Before garnering 29 interceptions in five years as an Eagle, he stole 21 in five years as a Ram. Philadelphia acquired him for a fifth-round pick in 1959.

3. Seth Joyner was an unheralded rookie linebacker out of Texas-El Paso. His drive and dedication far outpaced that of second-round pick Alonzo Johnson out of Florida, whose drug problems drove him out of the league.

4. Philadelphian Jess Richardson, who went from Roxborough High School to the University of Alabama and then back home when the Eagles picked him in the eighth round of the 1953 draft. He spent eight years as defensive tackle in Philadelphia and got special dispensation from the league to go without a face mask because he said that it would ruin his peripheral vision. After the popular Richardson was benched midseason in 1961, he hooked on with the Boston Patriots for three more seasons and appeared in the 1963 AFL title game. He did not wear a face mask in Boston either. Upon retiring, he coached the defensive line in Boston and Philly and died from kidney disease at the age of 45.

5. Carl Hairston got a job delivering furniture after high school and was spotted in a pool hall two years later by a recruiter for Maryland-Eastern Shore. Dick Vermeil selected him in the ninth round of his first draft in 1976, and he went on to have a 15-year NFL career in Philadelphia, Cleveland and Arizona.

6. John Bunting, who called the signals for Marion Campbell's tough, smart defensive units in the late 1970s, was cut by the Eagles in 1983 and caught on for two years as a player-coach with the Philadelphia Stars of the USFL with whom he finally won a title in 1984.

7. Arguably the greatest basketball player of all time, Michael Jordan. The quiet Simmons was used to being overshadowed, but the ninth-round draft pick fashioned a solid, 15-year career as an NFL starter in five cities, most notably Philadelphia.

8. Mel Tom was an undersized, active and outspoken defensive end who challenged defensive line coach Jerry Wampfler to a fight and quit the team in 1973, forcing a trade to Chicago. Wampfler was offensive line coach under Dick Vermeil and Marion Campbell and would have other run-ins with Eagle players.

9. Tom Brookshier was from Colorado and was a natural to assist Buck Shaw as he began the Air Force Academy football program. Three years later, Shaw came to the Eagles where Brookshier was a hard-hitting star defensive back.

10. A former Marine from West Chester, Chuck Weber was the middle linebacker while Chuck Bednarik was the team's center and sometime outside linebacker. Midway through the 1961 season, new coach Nick Skorich decided to shake up his slumping defense and moved Bednarik to the middle where he played for his last year and a half. Weber retired after the 1961 season.

 OVERTIME: *Uniform Number Question:* Ollie Matson played under Kuharich in college at San Francisco. In 1952, Matson was drafted by the Cardinals and became their first black player under new coach Joe Kuharich. In Philadelphia 12 years later, Kuharich traded for Matson, who played his last three years as an Eagle.

EAGLE KICKERS

1. Guard/kicker Cliff Patton set a league record by converting 84 consecutive extra points successfully from 1947 to 1949. He still holds the team record for most extra points in a season with 50 in 1948.

2. Bobby Walston became the NFL's all-time leading scorer in the last week of 1961 by passing Lou Groza of the Browns. Lou Groza had passed Don Hutson just the week before to become the all-time leader. The following season was Walston's last and he scored just 48 points; Groza scored 75 and blew past Walston for good.

3. Tom Dempsey in 1974 when he made 10 of 16 field goals and missed four of 30 extra points.

4. Horst Muhlmann in 1975 when he made 20 of 29 field goals and missed three of 29 extra points. Muhlmann was acquired for a draft pick, was a small improvement over Dempsey and was gone two years later.

5. Sam Baker scored 977 points in the NFL, but never more than 92 in a season. He spent five years in Washington, two each in Cleveland and Dallas, and six in Philadelphia. He was a good kicker for his time, but a better punter. Mark Moseley won the league MVP award in 1983 when he scored 161 of the 1,372 points he amassed in his long career as the last straight-ahead kicker in the NFL. He spent his rookie season in Philadelphia, two in Houston, 11½ in Washington and half a season in Cleveland.

6. Both were barefoot kickers, but Franklin was right-footed and McFadden was left-footed.

7. Although he had not yet passed George Blanda when he was in Philadelphia, Gary Anderson is the all-time leading scorer with 2,434 points.

8. The Eagles tried to replace Walston as kicker with Dick Bielski in 1955, but Bielski only managed to make nine of 23 field-goal attempts that year. After that, they used him only for field-goal attempts beyond Walston's range, and he missed all eight attempts from 1956 to 1959. Bielski also failed to replace Walston as tight end in 1957-58, and was selected by Dallas in the 1960 expansion draft.

9. Actually it was only once, but it was odd nonetheless. With five seconds left in the second half of a game against the Bucs in 1999, everyone on the Eagle field-goal unit was lined up on the field except for the kicker, normally reliable veteran kicker Norm Johnson. Johnson raced on the field at the last second and then missed the rushed 26-yard attempt.

10. Punter Rick Engles made a public stink in 1978 when he claimed that Dick Vermeil told him to fake an injury so he could go on injured reserve. The NFL took away an Eagles draft pick to punish them for stashing players. Engles never punted again in the NFL, ending his three-year career with a weak 38.4 average.

OVERTIME: *Uniform Number Question:* Linebacker Lee Roy Caffey wore 34 as a rookie in 1963. He and a number one draft pick (who would turn out to be Donny Anderson) were traded to Green Bay in 1964 for center Jim Ringo and fullback Earl Gros, who took Caffey's number in Philadelphia. Neither player wore 34 at any of their other stops in the NFL.

QUIZ ANSWERS !!!!

SECTION IV
MANAGEMENT

OWNERSHIP

1. Jerry Wolman made a fortune in construction, but overextended his finances with too many purchases and investments so that when his construction business ran into trouble, he could not pay his ongoing debts. Bankrupt, he was forced to sell the team to trucking millionaire Leonard Tose. Tose liked high living and strove for his money to run out at the same time he ran out of breath. Due to a miscalculation likely induced by alcohol, he went bankrupt first.

2. Although Jeff Lurie may have wanted to, only the first two Eagle owners went to Ivy League schools: Bert Bell to Penn and Lex Thompson to Yale.

3. Thompson sold the team in 1949 to a local group of 100 Philadelphia investors who each put up $3,000 to buy the team. Led by Democratic City Chairman James Clark, they were known as the "100 Brothers." When they sold out to Jerry Wolman in 1963, the "brothers" were down to about 60 members.

4. Art Rooney sold the Pittsburgh franchise to Lex Thompson and bought a half share of the Eagles from his friend Bert Bell after the 1940 season. He missed Pittsburgh so much that he and Bell convinced Thompson to switch cities with them a couple months later.

5. Paul Brown was forced out of the Browns in 1962 by Art Modell and tried to bring together an investment group to buy the Eagles from the "brothers" the next year.

6. Lex Thompson graduated from Yale in 1936, the same year he went to the Olympics as part of the U.S. field hockey team. Three years later he competed in the world bobsled championships in Italy.

7. Although Jerry Wolman lost his seven-year lawsuit to buy back the Eagles from Leonard Tose in the 1970s, he eventually not only righted his financial plight, but rebuilt his fortune to the degree that he was a serious bidder for the Redskins in 1999.

8. Bert Bell was a definite man about town in his younger days before he bought the franchise, but the two owners who engaged in the high life while owning the team were Lex Thompson and Leonard Tose. Thompson was only 26 when he bought the team and had a reputation for dating Hollywood starlets. He served in the Army during World War II and was married three times. Five years after he sold the team in 1954, he had to interrupt his honeymoon with his third wife to testify in a paternity suit brought against him. Sadly, he would die a few months later at the young age of 39. Tose liked the ladies, gambling and drinking. He went through an immense fortune in just a few years by gambling as much as $100,000 on a single hand of cards at nearby Atlantic City.

9. A group led by singer Frankie Laine wanted to buy the Eagles from Thompson and move them to San Francisco in 1949. In 1956, a bid from a Louisville group to move the team

to Kentucky was received by the "brothers." In 1984, Tose was struggling to hang onto the team as his finances drained away, and he considered moving the Eagles to Phoenix before Mayor Goode sweetened the local stadium deal. San Antonio has never expressed an interest in the Birds.

10. Blue-collar Philadelphia fans see Jeff Lurie's comment that the Eagles were the "gold standard" in the NFL before they have won a single Super Bowl as an elitist attitude that separates Lurie from them. It makes us question his commitment to winning a title despite his willingness to spend money on free agents and his skill in getting a beautiful new stadium erected.

 OVERTIME: *Uniform Number Question:* Fullback Ted Dean replaced the team's injured leading rusher Clarence Peaks midway through the season and made the key kick return in the championship that set up the winning touchdown that he also scored. A series of leg injuries kept Dean from realizing his full potential. The Radnor native taught school in the area for many years after his football career ended.

QUIZ ANSWERS 36

BERT BELL

1. Bert's father, John Cromwell Bell, was District Attorney of Philadelphia and then Attorney General for the state of Pennsylvania. His brother John was elected Pennsylvania's lieutenant governor, served briefly as governor and was named as a justice to the state's Supreme Court. In addition, his maternal grandfather Leonard Myers was a U.S. congressman from 1863 to 1875.

2. Bert played quarterback for the Quakers and in 1916 led Penn to the Rose Bowl where they lost to Oregon.

3. Bell took a year off to serve with a hospital unit in France during World War I before returning to Penn.

4. Legendary coach John Heisman, for whom the Heisman Trophy is named. Heisman, who had played for the Quakers in the 19th century, returned to coach the team from 1920 to 1922.

5. Before Bill Cosby, Bert chose Temple in 1929 to assist his teammate from prep school and college, Heine Miller. Bell coached the backfield for a few years in North Philly just as he had at Penn for eight years.

6. By 1936, the Eagle franchise had lost $80,000, so Bell bought out the other investors for $4,500. For the team's first three years, he had served as general manager, ticket seller and public relations agent. In 1936, he added head coach to his responsibilities, but it turned out that his weaknesses were in selecting and coaching players. The team was 9-21-1 under Lud Wray for three years and 10-44-2 in Bell's five years. Bell's winning percentage of .196 is the lowest of any Eagle coach in history. The bottom five are Bell, .196; Wayne Milner, .200; Jerry Williams, .258; Lud Wray, .306 and Hugh Devore, .313.

7. In 1929, Bell found himself $50,000 in debt from gambling, lavish spending and the stock market decline. His father bailed him out, and Bert gave up the gambling vice in return.

8. Why does any man do anything serious? For a woman. After he fell in love with Ziegfeld Follies star Frances Upton, Bert gave up drinking in 1932 and they got married in 1934.

9. Bell suffered a fatal heart attack at Franklin Field in 1959 while watching a game between his two former teams, the Eagles and Steelers, on the field where he had played quarterback 40 years before.

10. DeBenneville "Bert" Bell was given his grandmother's maiden name.

 OVERTIME: *Uniform Number Question:* Joe Muha was a crushing lead blocker on offense and a punishing tackler on defense. He led the NFL in punting in 1948 with a 47.3 average. Muha also kicked off for the Eagles and tried the occasional long field goal. In this last duty, he was not so effective, hitting only one of 16 field-goal attempts in his five-year career.

QUIZ ANSWERS 37
COACHES AND GMs

1. Wray had played and coached with Bell at the University of Pennsylvania and coached the Quakers to a 5-4 record in 1930.

2. Bo McMillin was forced to step down after the Birds won the first two games in 1951 because he had cancer. He died the next year. He had coached Eagle star Pete Pihos during his 14 years as coach of Indiana and had most recently coached the Detroit Lions before signing with the Eagles.

3. Hugh Devore and Buck Shaw played under Knute Rockne; Wayne Milner and Joe Kuharich played under Elmer Layden, who had been a member of the legendary Four Horsemen backfield and left Notre Dame to become NFL commissioner.

4. Offensive line coach Nick Skorich took over the team in 1961 and went 15-24-2 in three years, while defensive coach Jerry Williams came back from Canada to take over the Eagles in 1969 and went 7-22-2 in just over two seasons.

5. On the 1960 championship team, Marion Campbell and Ed Khayat were both starters on the defensive line. Khayat took over from Jerry Williams and lasted less than two years as head coach. Campbell took over from Dick Vermeil and lasted three inglorious seasons in Philadelphia.

6. Shaw would not take the job until the team had a veteran quarterback, so the Eagles traded for Norm Van Brocklin. Furthermore, Buck was an executive with a corrugated box company and worked the same arrangement he had when he coached the 49ers: he did not work in the off-season. In Philadelphia, Jerry Williams took care of most things during that time. Shaw was a master at delegating and that style worked for him as he built a champion team in Philly.

7. Pete Retzlaff was a great, hard-working player, but a disaster in the front office. When Leonard Tose gained control of the Eagles in 1969, he first offered Pete the head coaching job before hiring him as general manager. His drafts were weak, his trades were almost uniformly bad and his coaches were overmatched. He resigned after the 1972 season.

8. Zero. Georgia alumnus Campbell took over the Falcons in 1974 from his old teammate Norm Van Brocklin and went 6-19 in parts of three seasons. Three years in Philadelphia brought three more losing seasons, and yet the Falcons brought him back for three more losing seasons in 1987. His lifetime coaching record is 34-80-1.

9. Notre Dame alumnus Vince McNally served as GM for 15 years under the "100 Brothers."

10. Lurie hired eight different guys with overlapping terms and job responsibilities before Andy took complete control in 2000: Bob Wallace, Bob Ackles, Dick Daniels, John Wooten, Chuck Banker, Mike Lombardi, Bryan Broaddus and Tom Modrak.

 OVERTIME: *Uniform Number Question:* Tom Woodeshick's baseball pitcher cousin was Hal Woodeschick. Tom led the Eagles in rushing three times and was an underrated performer on some awful teams in the 1960s.

KUHARICH, KHAYAT AND KOTITE: THREE STRIKEOUTS

1. After losing to the Giants 62-10 on November 26, 1972, Ed Khayat's postgame assessment of the Eagles effort team ("All but a handful of [the players] quit") was no doubt accurate. The Birds were in the midst of a 2-11-1 season that would get both Khayat and GM Pete Retzlaff fired.

2. The president of the local chapter of the Meaningless Cliché Club, Rich Kotite, regularly praised his losing club by saying, "They left nothing in the locker room" after a game.

3. Mr. Malaprop, Joe Kuharich, may have had a third eye, but unfortunately he was blind in all of them.

4. Again Mr. Malaprop, Joe Kuharich, said it, but one could certainly envision, "We were three points behind, but that's not the same as being even" coming out of Rich Kotite's mouth to explain some failed strategy.

5. Back to Rich Kotite, who often began press conference replies with "without question" in a strong New Yawk accent.

6. Ed Khayat said, "Good grooming is one of the many facets of discipline" to defend his new policy of no facial hair for Eagles players in 1971.

7. Joe Kuharich rationalized the rare and unusual swapping of two NFL starting quarterbacks with "It's quite rare, but not unusual." The trade of Sonny Jurgensen for Norm Snead on April Fool's Day, 1964 was the first of many disastrous trades to come under Kuharich.

8. Joe Kuharich is still the only Fighting Irish coach to leave South Bend with a losing record. He also had losing records at each of his pro stops: the Cardinals, Redskins and Eagles. His one point of success in coaching was his first job at the University of San Francisco from 1948 to 1951. His 1951 team went 10-0 and featured nine future pro players, including Hall of Famers Ollie Matson, Gino Marchetti and Bob St. Clair. The publicity director for USF at the time was Pete Rozelle. Despite all this, USF dropped football in 1952 because it was losing money.

9. Midway through 1994, the Eagles were 7-2 and Kotite's career coaching record was 36-17. After dropping the last seven games that season, Kotite was fired but quickly snapped up by the Jets, whose ancient owner Leon Hess declared, "I want to win now." Richie took the Jets to a 3-13 season followed by 1-15 before being fired with a 4-28 record in his hometown. In his last 39 games as a head coach, Kotite went 4-35 to end up with a lifetime 40-52.

10. Kuharich turned "fine kettle of fish" into "fine kennel of fish," "horse of a different color" into "horse of a different fire department," and "now the shoe is on the other foot" into "now the shoe is on the other side of the table."

OVERTIME: *Uniform Number Question:* Independent kicker and punter Sam Baker did not get along with intense winning football coaches like Paul Brown and Tom Landry and so washed out of Cleveland and Dallas quickly, but he found a home for eight years with Joe Kuharich.

QUIZ ANSWERS 39
BUDDY RYAN AND DICK VERMEIL

1. Buddy's cutting and unfair reference was to Harry Gamble, the team's GM, as the "illegitimate son" of imperious owner Norman Braman, "that guy in France."

2. The team's leading rusher in 1985 was Earnest Jackson who gained 1,000 yards but only averaged 3.6 yards per carry. Buddy was so eager to unload him he said, "I'd trade him for a six pack and it wouldn't even have to be cold." That comment, while funny, did nothing for Jackson's trade value and Ryan finally cut him. The Steelers picked him up, and he played three seasons in Pittsburgh. In Buddy's first four years as coach, the leading rusher among Eagle running backs averaged 3.3, 3.7, 3.4 and 3.4 yards per carry until finally Heath Sherman averaged 4.2 in 1990.

3. Evidently trying to throw everyone off the scent, Buddy declared Byars, who had a foot problem in college, a medical reject and then picked him.

4. When Ryan cut Cris Carter, he made the strange comment, "All he can do is catch touchdowns." It was only later that it came out that Carter had drug problems and that Buddy compassionately was trying to give him a chance to straighten out his life.

5. A. "We believe in giving everybody a chance. This is America, not Russia." Alonzo Johnson had had drug problems in college, but Buddy picked him anyway in the second round. Johnson flubbed his chance when he couldn't stay away from the drugs. B. "He looks like a reject guard from the USFL. He's so fat." Michael Haddix was a large, slow fullback left over from the Marion Campbell era. Unexpectedly, he remained on the team for three years under Buddy. C. "He wasn't blocking in any of the drills. I assumed when the linebackers started blitzing, he'd leave." Herman Hunter was another carryover from Campbell, but he left training camp in Buddy's first year and prompted this comment. Hunter played two more nondescript years in Detroit and Houston.

6. Dick Vermeil was the first special teams coach in the NFL with the Rams under George Allen. Vermeil's attention to detail made him a natural for that post, and his extreme work ethic was a match for the supremely dedicated Allen.

7. Quarterback John Sciarra threw second-half touchdown passes of 16 and 67 yards to wide receiver Wally Henry to beat Ohio State. The undersized Sciarra was drafted in the fourth round by the Bears, but did not make the team; the undersized Henry was not even drafted. Henry made Vermeil's Eagles as a free agent receiver in 1977, and Sciarra came on board in 1978. The two former Bruins took turns with the punt-returning duties over the next few seasons.

8. The Eagles didn't have a first-round draft pick for five years because of Mike McCormack's ill-fated trades. In Vermeil's first year, 1976, his highest draft choice was a number four that he used on defensive end Mike Smith; he didn't have a number one (or a number two) until 1979 when he picked Jerry Robinson, a linebacker he had recruited to UCLA. Robinson went on to be a very solid performer for the Birds and Raiders.

9. Carl Hairston played seven years under Vermeil and one more under Marion Campbell before he was traded to Cleveland for a ninth-round pick. He played seven more years in the NFL. When Vermeil returned to coaching in St. Louis, Carl was one of a core of former players he added to his staff. In fact, when Vermeil later moved on to Kansas City, Carl came with him again. He and front-office executive Lynn Stiles are the two men who have been with Vermeil for every one of his NFL victories.

10. During his first training camp, Vermeil complained that a local fireworks extravaganza celebrating the nation's Bicentennial was a disruption and wanted it stopped.

 OVERTIME: *Uniform Number Question:* Philadelphia native Bill Mackrides led the country in passing at the University of Nevada in 1946. The backup quarterback most notably earned his keep filling-in for Tommy Thompson on October 24, 1948 and leading the Eagles to a 12-7 victory over the "Monsters of the Midway." It was the first time Philadelphia had ever beaten the Bears. Mackrides threw very few passes and ran out the clock himself with three quarterback keepers while the Bears tried unsuccessfully to force a fumble.

GREASY NEALE AND ANDY REID

1. Neale took an unheralded Washington and Jefferson team to the 1923 Rose Bowl where they tied the heavily favored California Bears 0-0. He also coached West Virginia Wesleyan, the University of Virginia and West Virginia University.

2. Neale spent eight seasons in the major leagues playing the outfield for the Cincinnati Reds and Philadelphia Phillies and compiled a .259 lifetime batting average. In the tainted 1919 World Series, Neale batted .357 for the victorious Reds. He only appeared in 16 games for the Phillies in 1921 before returning to the Reds the following year.

3. After the All-America Conference champions took apart the champion Eagles 35-10 in the opening football game of the 1950 season. The Eagles had never seen such well-executed timing patterns as the Browns ran, and Cleveland only rushed the ball 10 times in the first three quarters. Although the Browns spent the fourth quarter running out the clock, Neale was clearly perturbed by the game and made the basketball comment. Just to prove a point in the 1950 rematch, the Browns won 13-7 without passing the ball once.

4. As the new coach of the Eagles in 1941, Neale moved quickly to learn the Bears' T-Formation by obtaining a copy of the newsreel footage of Chicago's 73-0 thrashing of the Redskins in the 1940 title match. Greasy ran that film back and forth hours a day for months in Thompson's office to implement what he saw as the offense of the future.

5. Yes, once. In 1941, Neale's first year as coach, the Eagles ran the ball 59% of the time. In each of his other nine seasons as coach, Philadelphia ran the ball between 64% and 76%.

6. Reportedly, Reid spent over half an hour at his meeting with Jeff Lurie and Joe Banner going through all the details and permutations of long-snapping. It was obvious that Reid was methodical and attuned to detail.

7. Green Bay made Reid its assistant head coach in an attempt to keep another team from hiring him as offensive coordinator. If their longtime offensive coordinator, Sherman Lewis, had gotten a head coaching job, Reid probably would have replaced him. The Eagles changed all that by offering Andy a head coaching position even though he had never even been a coordinator.

8. When Reid told Owens it wasn't Eagle policy for a player to wear black spandex tights in practice, Owens made a bet with Reid that he would catch 15 touchdown passes. If he did, Reid agreed that not only would he allow Owens to wear the tights, but also Andy would model a pair himself. It was a *GQ* cover waiting to happen, but Owens' injury ended his season at 14 touchdowns.

9. Andy Reid played on the offensive line in front of Jim McMahon in 1979 and 1980 at BYU. McMahon played in Philadelphia from 1990 to 1992 and then hooked up again with Reid in 1995-96 in Green Bay where Reid was coaching tight ends and McMahon was finishing his career as a backup to Brett Favre.

10. Reid coached under LaVell Edwards at BYU in 1982, and one of the stars on the team was Philadelphia sportscaster and onetime Eagle Vai Sikahema.

OVERTIME: *Uniform Number Question:* Frank Reagan of the Penn Quakers spent four years with the Giants and led the NFL in interceptions with 10 in 1947. He joined the Eagles as a defensive back in 1949 and stayed three years. In 1954, he became the head football coach at Villanova, but could only manage a 17-36 record in six years.

QUIZ ANSWERS

TRADES

1. The Redskins also sent defensive back Claude Crabb to the Eagles for Jimmy "Gummy" Carr. Crabb had picked off nine passes in his first two years in Washington, but had no interceptions in two years in Philadelphia and was traded to the Rams for a seventh-round pick. Carr played two more years in Washington where he shifted to linebacker before going into coaching.

2. Kuharich tried to interest Minnesota coach Norm Van Brocklin in trading Fran Tarkenton for Norm's former teammate since Tarkenton's scrambling drove the Dutchman crazy, but Van Brocklin was not persuaded.

3. The Vikings sent Philadelphia tackle Steve Smith, who played for the Eagles for four years along with second-, third- and sixth-round draft picks. The second-round pick was used on Hank Allison, who played two years as a guard for the Birds.

4. Kuharich obtained kicker/punter Sam Baker and two journeyman linemen, John Meyers and Lynn Hoyem, from the Cowboys.

5. The Eagles gave up Pro Bowl tackle Buck Lansford and second-year defensive back Jimmy Harris in addition to the top draft pick. Harris had been the quarterback on the Oklahoma Sooner teams that featured Tommy McDonald and played only a season in

LA before going to Dallas in the expansion draft. Lansford played three seasons in LA before retiring. The draft choice turned out to be Dick Bass, who was an undersized leading rusher for the Rams for a decade.

6. Bert Bell, who lobbied so hard to have a common player draft adopted by the NFL, ended up trading the rights to four of his six number one picks from 1936 to 1941 to the Bears in separate deals for a plethora of bodies. The Bears obtained the rights to Jay Berwanger, Sam Francis and Tommy Harmon, who didn't work out, as well as George McAfee, who went on to the Hall of Fame. The Bears also obtained the rights to Hall of Famer Sid Luckman from Pittsburgh in such a deal.

7. From the Rams, the Eagles got ineffectual three-year linebacker Fred Brown, one-year tackle Frank Molden and a third-round draft choice the Eagles used on injury-prone runner Harry Wilson.

8. Trader Joe Kuharich happily complied with Cross' demand two months later. The Rams gave up receiver Willie Brown, whom Kuharich termed "versatile," and Aaron Martin, whom Joe said was "one of the finest defensive backs in the NFL." Brown lasted half a season and Martin lasted two. Martin had one 67-yard punt return for a touchdown, but was continually beaten deep as a cornerback. Three years later, Pete Retzlaff brought Cross back for one more year as part of a terrible trade of disgruntled Hall of Fame tackle Bob Brown to the Rams.

9. Wilbert was sent to the Lions for serviceable linebacker Garry Cobb, who has since made a name for himself in the area as a broadcaster. Montgomery retired after a season in Detroit.

10. Green Bay had drafted tackle John Michels number one in 1996, and he was a flop; the following season, Ray Rhodes made a disastrous reach with his top pick and selected spindly defensive end Jon Harris. What to do? With former Packer assistant Andy Reid coaching in Philadelphia and former Eagle coach Rhodes coaching Green Bay, a flop swap was made so that neither team would have to suffer the ignominy of cutting its own number one pick. Both players appeared in 24 games with their original teams and 0 with their new clubs.

 OVERTIME: *Uniform Number Question:* Randy Logan lasted 11 years in Philadelphia and never missed a game, recording 23 interceptions as a defensive leader.

FREE AGENCY

1. Perennial All-Pro and unparalleled tough guy Bucko Kilroy played guard and tackle on offense and defense for 13 years from 1943, when he came to the Eagles as a free agent from Temple, to 1955, when he went down with a knee injury that effectively ended his career. He went into scouting and was still employed by the Patriots when they defeated the Eagles in Super Bowl XXXIX, a career of over 60 years in the NFL.

2. In Super Bowl XXXIX against New England, Greg Lewis caught a 30-yard score that brought the Eagles within a field goal in the last two minutes. The undersized Lewis got a chance to start in 2005 and proved himself an able number four receiver, not a number one or two.

3. Herman Edwards signed with the Eagles in 1977 and led the team with six interceptions as a rookie. Edwards was an all-around cornerback who played both the pass and the run well. Although not extremely fast, he was smart, disciplined, tough and durable enough that he started all 135 games in his nine-year Eagle career. Herm finished as the second leading interceptor in team history with 33 and had five more in seven playoff games.

4. Bill Cowher was undrafted out of North Carolina State in 1979 and was the last linebacker cut by Dick Vermeil in training camp. After Cowher caught on with Cleveland, he served as captain of the Browns' special teams. The Eagles spent a ninth-round draft pick to reacquire Cowher, who was called "Face" for his long jaw and intensity. His Steelers won Super Bowl XL in 2006.

5. South Philly's Vince Papale was short on talent, but long on desire. He attended Saint Joseph's University, which did not have a football team, and then went into teaching. In 1974, he hooked on as a receiver with the Philadelphia Bell of the World Football League. When the Eagles held open tryouts in 1976, this 30-year-old school teacher impressed Dick Vermeil enough that Vince was given a chance to come to training camp. Papale played three years as a special teams demon for the rebuilding Eagles. He was the real Rocky and his story has been made into a 2006 movie starring Mark Wahlberg, best known for *Boogie Nights* and *The Italian Job*.

6. Greg Brown dropped out of Eastern Illinois and was working construction in Washington, D.C. to support his family in 1981. His former college defensive line coach called Eagles defensive line coach Chuck Clausen, who agreed to bring Brown in. Brown was undersized, but hungry in more ways than one; he gained 25 pounds by the end of training camp and made the team. By his third season, he became a starter under new head coach Marion Campbell and the next year, 1984, he led the team with 16 sacks. Brown parlayed that into a new three-year, $1.5 million contract.

7. While Keith Jackson was holding out for a new contract in 1992, an antitrust lawsuit by the Jets' Freeman McNeil was being heard and the jury struck down the NFL's existing

Plan B free agency program. Jackson and three other NFL holdouts at the time (Webster Slaughter, D.J. Dozier and Garin Veris) were given a five-day window by the judge to sign as free agents with any team they chose. Jackson, an All-Pro tight end, signed with the Dolphins, and the flood of Eagle free agents would follow Keith out of town.

8. The Eagles signed Tim Harris, who most recently had been the pass-rushing specialist who had tried to replace Charles Haley with the 49ers. After a four-game zero-sack 1993 with Philadelphia, Harris returned to San Francisco for their 1994 Super Bowl team. At his best as a young blitzer in Green Bay, Harris was a one-dimensional player, vastly different than Hall of Famer Reggie White.

9. Seth Joyner, Clyde Simmons and Andre Waters all fled Philadelphia while Braman still owned the team. In April 1994, Jeff Lurie bought the Birds and the atmosphere changed immediately. The Eagles managed to upgrade each of the lost positions with William Fuller and Burt Grossman at defensive end, Bill Romanowski at linebacker, and Greg Jackson and Mike Zordich at safety. All were upgrades over the departed aging Eagles at that stage of their careers.

10. In 1999, Reid brought in Charles Johnson and Torrance Small. In 2001, he signed James Thrash from the Redskins. In 2004, the Eagles originally did sign Terrell Owens as a free agent, but the 49er contract snafu forced them to trade for him, so that doesn't count. In 2005, Darnerian McCants was more of a street pickup than a free-agent signing. In 2006, Reid signed Jabbar Gaffney of the Texans. There was a bidding war for none of these wide outs.

 OVERTIME: *Uniform Number Question:* Keith Byars, who is famous as number 41, wore 42 as a rookie because Earnest Jackson still held 41 (briefly). Byars switched to 41 and wore that for the rest of his career with four different teams.

QUIZ ANSWERS 43
THE DRAFT

1. The very first NFL draft choice was also the very first recipient of the Heisman Trophy, Jay Berwanger of the University of Chicago. However, Berwanger had no interest in playing professional football, either with the Eagles who drafted him or with the Bears who later acquired his rights. Not only did Berwanger never play pro football, but neither did any of the Eagles' other eight draft choices in 1936.

2. In 1949, the NFL instituted the Bonus Choice system where the very first selection in the draft was awarded in a drawing. This was another idea of Bert Bell's, and the first drawing was won by the champion Eagles, who selected Chuck Bednarik with their bonus pick. With their own first pick at the end of the first round, they selected Notre Dame quarterback Frank Tripucka. It might have worked out better had they chosen Norm Van Brocklin or George Blanda, two Hall of Famers who were also available. The Eagles waived Tripucka early in the season, and the Lions picked him up. He bounced around the NFL and CFL in the next decade before winding up his career with Denver of the AFL from 1960 to 1963. The Broncos even retired his number for leading Denver to no winning seasons and throwing 51 touchdowns against 85 interceptions in four years.

3. Drake tailback Johnny Bright was the first black player the Eagles ever selected number one; however, Bright elected to play in Canada. Midway through his senior year at Drake, Johnny was leading the nation in offense for the third straight season when Drake played Oklahoma A&M (now Oklahoma State) in a Missouri Valley Conference game. During the game, Bright had his jaw fractured by a vicious blow delivered by Wilbanks Smith well behind where the ball was and after the play had ended. Bright threw a touchdown pass on the next play before being forced to leave the game. Two newspaper photographers captured the incident in a sickening sequence of photos that made the cover of *Life* and won them the Pulitzer Prize. Drake pulled out of the conference over the incident, and Bright missed two games before returning for the season finale. Bright decided he did not want to be the Eagles' first black player and did not want to play in the NFL, but instead went north and became the CFL's all-time rushing leader. The 5'10", 225-pound halfback would have been an ideal replacement for the banged-up Steve Van Buren.

4. While Mitchell flopped as both a defensive and offensive lineman, first with the Eagles and then the Falcons, the Eagles could have picked either Howie Long (from Villanova!) or Mike Singletary and had a Hall of Famer.

5. If the Eagles wanted a Hall of Fame quarterback, they could have taken Jim Kelly or Dan Marino. If they wanted a Hall of Fame lineman who would last for 20 years, they could have taken Bruce Matthews. If they wanted a Hall of Fame cornerback with world-class speed, they could have taken Darrell Green. Or if they really wanted a running back, they could have settled for All-Pro Roger Craig.

6. For those who have blotted these four fat flops out of mind, Leonard Renfro was a defensive tackle, so he failed on the defensive (not offensive) line like the other three.

7. If the Eagles wanted a tackle, they could have taken All-Pro Jim Lachey from Ohio State. Also available was the greatest receiver in NFL history, Jerry Rice.

8. The Eagles passed up Warren Sapp, Hugh Douglas, Derrick Brooks and Ty Law to grab the disappointing Mamula.

9. In 1982, both the Eagles and the Buffalo Bills were in need of a wide receiver come draft time. Dick Vermeil mentioned to his friend Chuck Knox, who coached Buffalo, that Philadelphia liked Clemson's Perry Tuttle. The Bills surprised the Eagles with a last-

minute draft-day trade to jump past Philadelphia and secure Tuttle. The Eagles then went with Mike Quick, the favorite of their receivers' coach Dick Coury, on their turn. As it turned out, Tuttle caught only 24 passes in two injury-plagued seasons in Buffalo, while Quick became a five-time All-Pro and Pro Bowl player.

10. Johnny Green, a wiry pass rusher for Greasy Neale, was selected in the 16th round in 1944. Other late-round All-Pros include Russ Craft in the 15th round of 1943, Bobby Walston in the 14th round of 1951 and Norm Willey in the 13th round of 1950. However, since there were fewer teams in those days, rounds were shorter. For instance, Green was the 162nd player selected in 1944, but Walston was the 166th and Willey was 170th. Even more impressive was 1976 seventh-rounder Carl Hairston, who was 191st. The two All-Pros who went the longest both came in 1986: Seth Joyner in the eighth round and the 208th player picked, and Clyde Simmons in the ninth round and the 233rd player picked. One other player of note who never made All-Pro but was close to that level was John Bunting, a 10th-round pick in 1972 and the 248th player picked that year. To put that in perspective, there were only 255 selections made in the draft in 2006.

 OVERTIME: *Uniform Number Question:* In 1943, number 43, Jack Hinkle, was beaten for the rushing title by Bill Paschal of the Giants by one yard. Hinkle, who got his start with the Giants, claimed the official scorer had missed a long run he had against New York early in the season, but he lost his appeal. Hinkle had 571 yards rushing that season.

QUIZ ANSWERS !!!!

SECTION V
THE OFFBEAT

UNIFORM NUMBERS

1. Chuck Bednarik, Mr. Eagle, who played more seasons than any other Eagle, wore 60 in all 14 of them.

2. This distinction has been tossed back and forth between punters. Sean Landeta wore 7 as a 40-year-old in 2002, and then was exceeded by his injury replacement at the end of that season, 41-year-old Lee Johnson. When Landeta returned to Philadelphia in 2005 to replace injured Dirk Johnson, he wore 7 again but this time as a 43-year-old.

3. While 0 has never been worn, 92 has only been worn twice by Smiley Creswell for three games and then by Reggie White for whom it has been retired.

4. The top 10 in receptions through 2005 are Harold Carmichael, 589; Pete Retzlaff, 452; Pete Pihos, 373; Mike Quick, 363; Bobby Walston, 311; Fred Barnett, 308; Calvin Williams, 295; Tommy McDonald, 287; Ben Hawkins, 261 and Irving Fryar, 222. Carmichael wore 17, Retzlaff 44 and 25, Pihos 35, McDonald 25 and Hawkins 18. This list does not include the three running backs who are in the Eagles' overall top 10 for catches: Keith Byars, 371; Duce Staley, 275 and Wilbert Montgomery, 266.

5. The Eagles proposed that the NFL institute a numbering scheme by position. What they proposed was very similar to what the NFL later adopted in 1952 and stipulated that quarterbacks wore 10s, halfbacks wore 20s, fullbacks wore 30s, tailbacks wore 40s, centers wore 50s, guards wore 60s, tackles wore 70s and ends wore 80s. The Eagles stuck to this strictly for only one season, but followed it generally throughout the 1940s, while the NFL had no scheme and the All-America Conference devised their own. The AAC scheme was that centers wore 20s, guards wore 30s, tackles wore 40s, ends wore 50s, quarterbacks wore 60s, fullbacks wore 70s, and halfbacks wore 80s and 90s.

6. When Mike Ditka was traded to the Eagles from the Bears in 1967, his number, 89, was already taken by linebacker Mike Morgan, so Ditka reversed the numbers and wore 98. He switched back to 89 in 1968 when Morgan left.

7. Not until 1985 was 90 worn by an Eagle when linebacker Aaron Brown wore it.

8. Steve Van Buren, Chuck Bednarik and now Reggie White.

9. The Eagles have retired the numbers of four players not of Hall of Fame caliber, which is a high total. Jerome Brown's 99 was retired largely because of his tragic death. Al Wistert was a perennial All-Pro throughout the 1940s and conceivably still may make the Hall, and his 70 is retired. Two stars from the 1960s are retired more for sentimental reasons than anything else. Tom Brookshier was an excellent cornerback and team leader and has become a local institution, while Pete Retzlaff was an All-Pro at both split and tight end; 40 and 44, respectively, are retired in their honor.

10. While 13 has not been worn since 1978, the longest stretch in team history was for 2, which was worn by Joe Pilconis in 1934 and then went unworn until 1978 when Mike Michel wore it. This does not count numbers that had not been originated such as 90, which was not worn until 1985, as noted above.

 OVERTIME: *Uniform Number Question:* Defensive pass rusher Norm "Wild Man" Willey was drafted as a fullback and wore 44 in 1950-51. He switched to 63 in 1952 and then 86 from 1954 to 1957.

QUIZ ANSWERS 45

NICKNAMES

1. Kelley and Piro were both called "Whitey." Bassman, Kirkman, Mack, Ramsey and Weiner were all known as "Red." These players all played in Philadelphia more than 40 years ago.

2. Swede Elstrom and Swede Hanson were Eagle backs in the 1930s and Wayne "Big Swede" Robinson was an All-Pro linebacker in the 1950s.

3. All these nicknames are food-related: David "Doughboy" Alexander, Todd "Taco" Bell, Hank "Honey Buns" Fraley, Al "Cheeseburger" Harris and Ed "Eggs" Manske. Yes, Honey Buns is a stretch to claim a food connection, but let's keep it clean here.

4. Eric "Flea"Allen, Walter "Piggy" Barnes, Frank "Wild Horse" Emmons, Bobby "Goose" Freeman, Alan "Rabbit" Keen, Joe "Big Bird" Lavender, John "Bull" Lipski, George "Moose" Rado and Al "Big Ox" Wistert. Second, John Magee was called "Hog Jaw."

5. Reggie White and Pete Pihos. Actually with White it was "Big Dawg," but that's close enough. White was also called the "Minister of Defense," while Pihos was also called the "Golden Greek."

6. Greg "Trash" Garrity, Bill "Stinky" Hewitt, Earle "Greasy" Neale and Andre "Dirty" Waters.

7. "Arkansas" Fred Barnett and Edwin "Alabama" Pitts are obvious. Clyde Scott was known as "Smackover" because that was the Arkansas town where he went to high school. Steve Van Buren had loads of nicknames and one was the "Barefoot Boy of the Bayou" because he didn't like to wear socks.

8. Billy "Bullet" Barnes, Ed "Bibbles" Bawel, Ron "Bye Bye" Blye and Bob "Boomer" Brown. Bawel was somehow pronounced "Bobble," so his nickname was more than an alliterative mouthful. Blye's nickname was so apt for a speedster that it was a shame that he was such an ordinary player.

9. Norm "Dutchman" Van Brocklin, Bobby "Sheriff" Walston, Pete "Baron" Retzlaff, Don "Blade" Burroughs, Jimmy "Gummy" Carr, Marion "Swamp Fox" Campbell and Bobby "Cheewah" Walston (again). All were from the 1960 championship team. Ron "Polish Rifle" Jaworski, Dennis "Big Foot" Harrison, Carl "Big Daddy" Hairston, Charles "Home Boy" Smith and John "Frito Bandito" Bunting were all from the 1980 Super Bowl team.

10. David "Buddy" Ryan, Frank "Bucko" Kilroy, Lawrence "Buck" Shaw, Christian "Sonny" Jurgensen and Abisha "Bosh" Pritchard all had nicknames. Duce Staley and Smiley Creswell are their real names.

 OVERTIME: *Uniform Number Question:* Tom Brookshier wore 45 as a rookie in 1953. When he returned to the Eagles from two years of military service in 1956, he switched to 40 for the rest of his career, and the number was retired for him. After leaving the game, he had a long career in TV and radio, both locally and nationally. Vaughn Hebron, stylish broadcaster on the Eagles' postgame show, was a smallish running back and quick kick returner who wore 45 and then 20 with the Birds before finishing his career in Denver.

QUIZ ANSWERS 46

FAMILY CONNECTIONS

1. Dick Vermeil coached his nephew, special teams demon Louie Giammona, from 1978 to 1982.

2. With Ty Detmer as their sometime starter in 1997, the Eagles drafted his brother Koy in the seventh round of the draft. Koy spent 1997 on injured reserve while Ty finished his Eagle career, but both brothers were on the roster.

3. Ebert Van Buren followed his brother Steve to LSU, and the Eagles drafted him in the first round of the 1951 draft. He played with Steve in 1951, and played two more years beyond that, but had no impact on offense or defense.

4. Center Jim Pyne's grandfather George played tackle for Providence in 1931, and his father, George Pyne, Jr., played defensive tackle for the Patriots in 1965. While Jim Pyne appeared in only five games as an Eagle, he did play in the NFL for seven years.

5. Raleigh McKenzie played center for Philadelphia in 1995-96. He also spent 10 years in Washington and two each in Green Bay and San Diego. Meanwhile, his twin Reggie McKenzie spent five years in the NFL as a linebacker, mostly for the Raiders, before going into management in Green Bay.

6. Ed Khayat, who had started his career as a Redskin before playing with the 1960 Eagles champions, was traded (in 1962) back to Washington where he spent two seasons with his brother Bob, a kicker. Bob and Ed were both cut in 1964. Bob moved on with his life and eventually became chancellor at the University of Mississippi. Ed returned to the Eagles for two more seasons before finishing his career with the Patriots and then going into coaching. Both are members of the Mississippi Sports Hall of Fame.

7. The Eagles drafted George McAfee from Duke in the first round in 1940, but traded him to the Bears for the unforgettable Russ Thompson and Milt Trost. The next year, Pittsburgh drafted George's brother Wes in the 16th round, and Pittsburgh's draft became Philadelphia's in the franchise switch with Lex Thompson. Wes wore 40 in 1941 and ran the ball nine times for six yards, caught three passes for 30 yards, and completed one of four passes for four yards. George went to the Hall of Fame.

8. Matt Bahr's brother Chris kicked for the Bengals and Raiders; Nick Mike-Mayer's brother Steve kicked for four teams in six years; Luis Zendejas' brothers Joaquin and Max both kicked briefly in the NFL.

9. Don Looney led the NFL in receptions with 58 in 1940, catching passes from his college passer Davey O'Brien. He continued on with the Steelers after the franchise switch for two more uneventful seasons and later served as a field official in the league. His son Joe Don Looney attended two high schools, four colleges and played for four NFL teams in six seasons. He never lived up to his immense potential at any stop, but built a reputation as one of the most incorrigibly weird players in league history.

10. Tim Hasselbeck has not only been outshone by his quarterback brother Matt and his tight end father Don, but by his wife Elisabeth, a popular Survivor alum and a regular on daytime TV's *The View*.

 OVERTIME: *Uniform Number Question:* Izell "Toast" Jenkins was known for having a close-up view of many long touchdown passes by the opposition.

QUIZ ANSWERS 47

BIG HITS AND HITTERS

1. Norm "Wild Man" Willey broke Steeler quarterback Jim Finks' jaw on October 10, 1954 in a comeback 24-22 win. To show how tough Finks was, he not only played the following week, but also threw four touchdowns to upset the Browns 55-27. The newspaper accounts said Finks wore a makeshift mask that made him look like a man from Mars.

2. Hardy Brown was an undersized linebacker with a mean streak who tried to tackle everyone by taking a flying leap at them and driving his shoulder into their faces. In this game, he timed his hit perfectly and crushed Eagle halfback Toy Ledbetter's cheek. Ledbetter only missed two games that year, though.

3. Once again we must refer to the Chuck Bednarik hit on Frank Gifford in 1960. It was the quintessential Eagle moment captured in an unforgettable photo that depicts the apotheosis not only of Bednarik's career, but even of the whole Eagle franchise. That hit and photo reflected not only the toughness of Concrete Charlie, but of the Eagle franchise and its fans as well.

4. One series of photos accompanying the article shows Kilroy kneeing tackled Giant quarterback Arnold Galiffa in the back in a game in 1953. Galiffa suffered broken bones in his back and was done for the season.

5. It was speculated that the fine was $1,000, but it was announced only as "four figures." That sound ridiculous today, but at the time that could easily have been a month's salary.

6. Bergey was flying all over the field that night and made 18 tackles. The biggest was knocking the ball loose from Dennison on the 4 yard line in the second quarter where Joe Lavender picked it up and raced 96 yards for the only Eagle touchdown of the game. The Eagles pulled out a 13-10 win in the closing minute on a Tom Dempsey field goal, and Bill Bergey became an instant Philadelphia hero.

7. The "Body Bag Game" occurred on Monday night, November 12, 1990. In the pregame meeting, Buddy Ryan exhorted his Eagles to hit the Redskins so hard that they'd need to be carted out in body bags. In fact, 11 Redskins were knocked out of the game, including quarterbacks Stan Humphries and Jeff Rutledge.

8. Linebacker Jesse Small, a disappointing second-round pick in 1989, laid out former Eagle kicker Luis Zendejas in the "Bounty Bowl" on December 23, 1989. Jimmy Johnson later accused Buddy Ryan of putting cash bounties on the heads of Troy Aikman and Luis Zendejas. Fights erupted continually between the teams, and the league fined 10 Cowboys and seven Eagles for their participation. When the teams met again at the Vet 17 days later, snowballs rained down from the stands on the Cowboys and their coach, and several fights broke out on the field. The Birds won both games.

9. Simmons drove Troy Aikman into the ground on a sack on December 23, 1990 and separated the Cowboy's shoulder. Douglas tackled Bear quarterback Jim Miller hard after an interception in a 2002 playoff game and separated the Bear's shoulder. Douglas was fined $35,000.

10. On opening day, 2004, the Eagles beat up on the Giants, and returning Eagle favorite Jeremiah Trotter was in the process of winning his middle linebacker job back by playing special teams with gusto. On a punt return, he slammed into former Eagles punter Jeff Feagles, who was not looking, and decleated him. Feagles suffered a concussion and had his feathers ruffled, but continued in the game.

 OVERTIME: *Uniform Number Question:* Rich Kotite brought in hard-hitting safety Greg Jackson from the Giants to replace Andre Waters. Two years later, Ray Rhodes drafted Brian Dawkins to replace Jackson, who moved on to New Orleans.

QUIZ ANSWERS 48

FIGHTS ON AND OFF THE FIELD

1. NFL commissioner Bert Bell lived on the Main Line and ran into Kilroy's wife in town. She complained to him that she would be the one feeling the brunt of that fine. Bell made a deal with Mrs. Kilroy that if Bucko would stay out of trouble for the season, he would refund the fine. Bucko did, and Mrs. Kilroy got the $150 back.

2. Kilroy had kicked Charley Trippi out of bounds, so Trippi and some of his teammates let Kilroy feel the brunt of their helmets after the game. As is clear from these first two questions, Kilroy may have been the roughest, and some would say dirtiest, player in the league in his time.

3. Chuck got into it with another Chuck, Chuck Noll, after a rugged 16-0 Eagle loss to the Browns in November 1956. The fisticuffs were caught by a television camera and seen by Bert Bell, who fined Bednarik and ordered him to apologize to Noll.

4. Eagles Piggy Barnes and Chuck Bednarik and Steelers Frank Wydo and Charley Mehelich were all ejected from the game. One fight was between Bednarik and Wydo after Wydo took a cheap shot at Bednarik. Frank told Chuck it was payback for a hit Bednarik laid on Wydo in a game between Penn and Cornell the year before. After Wydo was traded to the Eagles in 1952, he and Concrete Charlie roomed together.

5. Bobby Walston was scrappy and tough. At least three times, he was ejected from games in the 1950s for fighting. In the 1953 opener against San Francisco, his battle with 49er Charley Powell escalated into a fourth-quarter free-for-all. In October 1955, Bobby was caught pummeling Redskin Dick Alban on the sidelines. Finally, in 1959, he got into it with the Cardinals' Carl Brettschneider.

6. In an act of foreshadowing, Philly fans pelted the Giants with snowballs just as they would the Cowboys 35 years later in the rematch after the "Bounty Bowl."

7. At a team harmony meeting on the Saturday evening after the assassination, there was some talk of not playing Sunday's game at all despite the commissioner's ruling. Defensive end Bill Quinlan was upset that that "guinea bastard" Pete Rozelle was making teams play. Cornerback Ben Scotti took immediate offense at the ethnic slur. Quinlan's roommate, defensive tackle John Mellekas, told Scotti to cool off, and teammates had to separate the two. After the meeting ended, Mellekas was putting money in a vending machine in the hall when the 180-pound Scotti knocked down the 250-pound lineman with a sucker punch and continued pounding Mellekas until he was pulled off. Ironically, the two ended up in adjoining rooms in the hospital for three days. Mellekas needed several stitches to close facial cuts and lost a tooth; Scotti severed a tendon in his finger on Mellekas' teeth while punching him. The Eagles waived Scotti and fined Mellekas $500.

8. After a *Monday Night Football* game against the 49ers in which there were over 60 fights in the stands and one fan set off a flare gun in the Vet, the Eagles arranged with the city to have Judge Seamus P. McCaffrey in session during games to deal with rowdy drunks and miscreants.

9. Half an hour before game time, Trotter was taunting several Atlanta players near the Falcon symbol in the middle of their field when Kevin Mathis came over and slugged Jeremiah. Officials reviewed videotape of the incident and threw both players out of the game before it started, which was a much bigger loss to the Eagles than the Falcons.

10. Hugh Douglas, who was Owens' teammate in 2004 and was now serving as "team ambassador," came into the locker room and made a thinly veiled comment about players with phony injuries. Owens took offense and they briefly fought before being separated.

 OVERTIME: *Uniform Number Question:* Jon Ritchie's helmet caused two large bumps to form on his forehead. The bumps resembled horns and sometimes bled.

ILLEGAL EAGLES

1. All three had violent encounters in their lives, but only Ramsey survived his. Alabama Pitts gained fame in the 1930s starring on the baseball team at Sing Sing where he was serving five years for armed robbery. When he was released in 1935, Eagles owner Bert Bell signed the speedy Pitts, and he played in three games as a back for the Birds. Six years later, he was stabbed to death in a bar in a dispute over a woman. Defensive back Roy Barni was traded to Washington in 1955. In 1957, the former Eagle intervened in a barroom fight and was shot and killed in the melee. Ramsey was shot on a street corner in West Philly during the 1970 season, but he recovered and played football again.

2. The Eagles announced in 1941 that they would give a tryout each year for one athletic convict of at least 6' and 200 pounds. Don McGregor, a 27-year-old who played in the backfield in an Iowa state prison while doing time for auto theft, was given a shot in 1943, but did not make the team.

3. Dempsey fled the country initially, but returned, was convicted of grand theft and served a year in prison in the 1960s.

4. Safety Ed Hayes did not win his $525,000 antitrust suit in 1970 against the Eagles in which he alleged that Philadelphia would not pay him after being injured and was slandering him to other teams. Reggie White did win his 1993 antitrust suit, but it was against the NFL, not the Eagles. In 1969, lineman Don Chuy was injured, and the Eagles claimed he had a rare blood condition and should give up football. Chuy sued for his remaining two years salary because the condition was due to his playing injury. A jury awarded Chuy $60,000 in back pay and $70,000 in damages in 1976.

5. Bullyboys Bucko Kilroy and linebacker Wayne Robinson sued *Life* over a photo essay called "Savagery on Sundays" about the level of violence in the NFL. In the piece, Robinson was described as punching and kicking Cleveland players, and Kilroy was described as the "toughest" and "orneriest" of the roughnecks in the league. The text declared that the Giants got Bucko back for injuring Arnold Galiffa by wrecking his knee on a "bootsy" play in 1955. Actually, Kilroy was injured when teammate Frank Wydo fell on his knee. Robinson and Kilroy filed a $250,000 libel suit, and two and a half years later, in April 1958, they won a $23,000 judgment in the eight-day trial held in Philadelphia. Both players were out of the NFL by then.

6. Dick Vermeil cut starter Mike Hogan and teammate James Betterson in 1978 after they were arrested on drug charges for which they were later cleared. Hogan returned to the Eagles in 1980 as a backup.

7. First-round draft pick Kevin Allen was convicted of rape at the Jersey shore, served three years in prison, and never played again. Chris Buckhalter, the older brother of Correll, was sentenced to 20 years in Mississippi for manslaughter.

8. Williams played one year and then was suspended by the league for smoking marijuana and never even petitioned the league to return. Johnson had trouble with drugs in college, could not stay away from them in the pros, and washed out of the league in two years. Terrence Carroll was arrested for smoking dope in his car on a street in South Philly with two teammates. Carroll was the only one charged and never played in the NFL.

9. In 1976, defensive end Blenda Gay was fatally stabbed in the neck by his wife while the 26-year-old was sleeping. His wife was found not guilty by reason of insanity and has been institutionalized ever since.

10. McNabb and Trotter were found guilty of parking in handicapped spots in Glassboro, N.J., although neither player was driving his vehicle at the time. They were just two of 400 such cases brought by a local activist who photographs cars parked illegally in handicapped areas.

 OVERTIME: *Uniform Number Question:* Jerry Williams played both running back and cornerback for the Eagles before coaching their defense and ultimately the whole team. It was the Peter Principle in action: a good assistant rose to his level of incompetence.

 Quiz Answers

INJURIES, BAD LUCK AND WHAT MIGHT HAVE BEEN

1. Mike Quick. In the five years before his body started breaking down, Quick averaged 62 catches and 11 TDs. He finished with 363 catches for 61 scores, but would have broken all Eagle receiving records if he could have stayed healthy.

2. Sonny Jurgensen's shoulder separation in the meaningless 1961 Playoff Bowl between second-place clubs was described by the team doctor as the worst he had ever seen. Jurgensen would have great years again, but they would be in Washington.

3. In a late-season game against Chicago, defensive leader Tom Brookshier was whipsawed between two Bears and his leg was broken so severely that he would never come back to play again, although he tried for two years. When Joe Theisman's leg was broken on *Monday Night Football* by Lawrence Taylor, it reminded many Eagle fans of Brooky's injury.

4. Randall Cunningham tore up his knee after being hit low by Bryce Paup of the Packers in the 1991 opener, and the team would miss the playoffs despite going 10-6. Cunningham won the Comeback Player of the Year award in 1992, and the Eagles won their first playoff game. The Birds started off 4-0 in 1993, but Cunningham broke his leg in the fourth game and the team finished 8-8. Cunningham would be gone from Philadelphia two years later, but would have one last great year throwing bombs to Randy Moss for Minnesota in 1998.

5. While tackling former SMU teammate Eric Dickerson, Wes Hopkins wrecked his knee early in 1986. He missed the rest of that year and all of 1987 rehabilitating his knee while Buddy built a hard-hitting, fearsome defense. Buddy never warmed up to Wes after he came back, although he was a Ryan-type safety who loved to hit and was popular with the fans.

6. Steve Van Buren's career had been in serious decline for two years due to the foot injuries and was about done when he was caught in a pileup in training camp. His knee was twisted at such an odd angle that coach Frank Reagan immediately got sick. It would take Van Buren two years just to be able to walk right again.

7. Damon Moore turned down a contract extension in 2001, and then tore knee ligaments in the playoffs and was released. Earlier that year, he was in the news for abandoning his Rottweiler puppy by tying it to a tree by a soccer field after his girlfriend told him the dog had to go. The Bears signed Moore, but he failed a drug test, was suspended and then released again. The next year, he washed out of the Arena League.

8. Andy Harmon was a popular, undersized overachiever who tore up his knee in the 1996 preseason. He got into two games late that season and five in 1997 before being forced to retire.

9. Small, rangy and quick defensive end Derrick Burgess missed all but one game with foot and Achilles injuries in 2002 and 2003. He finally got healthy for the 2004 season, but missed the last four games with a chest problem. He returned and had a terrific conference championship against Atlanta. In the off-season, though, he signed a rich free-agent contract with the Raiders. In 2005, he played in all 16 games for the first time since he was a rookie and led the NFL in sacks with 16.

10. Jerome Brown crashed his sports car in the summer of 1991 and had his number retired later that season.

 OVERTIME: *Uniform Number Question:* James Willis, brought along by Ray Rhodes from Green Bay, moved on to the Seahawks in 1999 under former coach Mike Holmgren. After a season in Seattle, Willis ended up as the leading tackler in the one year of the bizarre XFL.

T.O. AND OTHER NONCONFORMISTS

1. T.O. made this typically classy accusation that his former quarterback Jeff Garcia was gay to *Playboy*. That is ironic because Garcia was dating the *Playboy* Playmate of the Year at the time.

2. Dynamite Dave Smukler had dropped out of Temple after a dispute with the administration and could not get along in the pros either. He quit after the 1939 suspension and went to work in a glove factory. The Eagles traded him to Detroit, but he enlisted in the Army instead. After he got out of the service, he played in two games with the Boston Yanks before being suspended again. The Steelers and Rams later gave him tryouts, but he never played in the NFL again.

3. A flapping chinstrap will always bring to mind speedy receiver Ben Hawkins, who was the essence of a hip 1960s playboy bachelor.

4. Ricky Watters got the ball more than anyone in the league, and yet felt he was not seeing the pigskin enough. In one memorable incident, Watters' girlfriend chastised offensive coordinator Jon Gruden for failing to get her man the ball an adequate amount of the time.

5. Rangy Ernie Calloway was a 6'6", 250-pound defensive lineman picked in the second round of the draft. Known as "Spiderman," he was a talkative, undersized underachiever who once left training camp three times in one month in 1972. In 1973, he was traded along with Leroy Keyes to the Chiefs for Gerry Philbin, but did not make the team.

6. Tim Rossovich, who roomed with Steve Sabol of NFL Films during his crazy time in Philadelphia. Rossovich was something of a 1960s flower child off the field, but on the field he was an intense hitter who started out at defensive end before being moved to middle linebacker, which was a better fit for him. He and Bill Bradley held out of training camp in 1972, and Rossovich found himself traded to San Diego where he wrecked his knee.

7. Randall Cunningham was a world-class pouter. He was upset when Buddy Ryan lifted him for one series of a playoff game in 1990, but when he lost his starting job in 1994 to Bubby Brister, he figured he was done in Philadelphia. He cleaned out his locker and pouted on the sidelines, wearing his jacket inside out. New coach Ray Rhodes tried with new offensive coordinator Jon Gruden to reach him in 1995, but Randall once again lost his starting job to a quarterback of lesser skills, Rodney Peete, and wasn't much use to the team for the rest of the season. He retired after the season, but came back a year later with the Vikings.

8. Seth Joyner was a Buddy Ryan loyalist as well as being a glowering malignancy to new coach Rich Kotite. Eventually, Joyner extended his public barbs to his teammates, and

he, Clyde Simmons and Andre Waters fled to Buddy's haven in Arizona where they all found you can't live in the past.

9. This is a bit of a trick question since the back-flip touchdown celebration was Gizmo Williams' signature move in Canada. However, he only scored once in an exhibition game in Philadelphia, so he never got to dust off his move in an NFL game.

10. Moody, talented tight end Charles Young went from Charles as the NFL Rookie of the Year in 1973 to Charlie to Charli to Charle in his four years in Philadelphia. The Eagles traded him to the Rams for Ron Jaworski. Young played three years with the Rams, three with the 49ers and three with Seattle. He won a Super Bowl in San Francisco and caught over 400 passes in the NFL.

OVERTIME: *Uniform Number Question:* Willie Thomas, who recorded 33 sacks and 18 interceptions, seven in 1995, in nine years as an Eagle. He finished his career as a Raider.

QUIZ ANSWERS

COLLEGES

1. The quarterback is Donovan McNabb, and the school is Syracuse. Piro's career was interrupted by World War II. Hinkle was a blocking back in college before nearly leading the NFL in rushing. Ringo was a Hall of Fame center and Walters an All-Pro tackle.

2. Rutgers, football machine on the Raritan. One other Scarlet Knight of note to Eagle fans was Frank Burns, who was drafted in the second round in 1949, but never played in the NFL. He went on to coach at Rutgers in the 1970s and is the last Rutgers football coach to leave New Brunswick with a winning record.

3. Penn State. However, the only Penn State alumnus we remember is that damn Joe Jurevicius.

4. They all chose Temple: Hanson in the 1920s, Reese and Smukler in the 1930s, Kilroy and Jarmoluk in the 1940s, and Colman in the 1960s.

5. Vince Papale, as everyone knows, went to St. Joe's after the school had dropped football. Ted Laux and John Cole played for St. Joe's in the late 1930s. Mandarino and Somers went to La Salle in the 1930s and 1940s. None lasted more than a couple of years with the Eagles.

6. The game-breaker is Brian Westbrook, and the school is Villanova. Nick Basca was a small halfback who left the Eagles near the end of his rookie season to go into the service. Dave DiFillipo later coached the Pottstown Firebirds. Frank Budd was a world-class sprinter. Billy Walik was primarily a kick returner. Kevin Reilly is still on the Eagles' pregame radio show. Brian Finneran won the Walter Payton Award for the best I-AA player in the nation in 1997, just as Westbrook did in 2001.

7. Chuck Bednarik was a waist gunner in World War II and a Penn Quaker after it. Diddy Willson played briefly with the Eagles in the 1930s, as did Fran Murray who later broadcast the Birds' games on radio. Frank Reagan and George Savitsky played with Bednarik on the 1949 title team and Eddie Bell played with Chuck in the 1950s.

8. All attended West Chester. Weber was a good linebacker on the 1960 championship team. Kersey was a punter who liked snakes, and Ferko and Gersbach lasted one and two seasons, respectively.

9. All went to traditionally black colleges: Howell and Peoples to Grambling, Waters to Cheney State and Hairston to Maryland State.

10. All nine players chose not to go to college or were not able to. The only one to play on the team after 1950 was guard Dick Hart from 1967 to 1971. The only memorable players in the group are solid guard Duke Maronic and Philly's own star end Jack Ferrante from the back-to-back championship teams.

 OVERTIME: *Uniform Number Question:* Vic Lindskog from Stanford was a solid player, but continually outshone by Bears Hall of Famer Bulldog Turner in the 1940s.

QUIZ ANSWERS 53

MISCELLANEOUS

1. Marine Jack Sanders had played with Pittsburgh before the war and came back to play in four games with the 1945 Eagles with only part of his left arm.

2. In all, 104 Eagles served in World War II. Three players under contract to Philadelphia died without ever appearing in a game with the Birds: Alonzo Hearne, John O'Keefe and Alex Santelli. The two actual Eagles who died in the war were halfback Nick Basca and end Len Supulski, both of whom died in France in November 1944.

3. Buddy Ryan, Marion Campbell, Mike McCormack and Fred Bruney.

4. Bert Bell served in the ambulance corps in France in World War I. Jerry Wolman and Lex Thompson served in World War II.

5. Joe Kuharich, Wayne Millner and Jerry Williams. None of the three was a winner as an Eagle coach, but they were all winners as Americans.

6. Harold Wells served in the Army before attending Purdue in the early 1960s. When he came to the Eagles as a rookie, he was already a veteran.

7. Kevin Reilly was never more than a special teams performer and backup linebacker in his two years as an Eagle. After his brief playing career, he started experiencing a burning sensation in his shoulder. Over a two-year period, he underwent the knife three times and had his left shoulder and collarbone removed, as well as losing his left arm due to cancer.

8. Stan Baumgartner was the first beat reporter from the *Philadelphia Inquirer* to cover the Eagles in 1933. He went 6-11 in five seasons from 1914 to 1922 pitching for the Phillies; with the A's, he went 20-10 from 1924 to 1926.

9. Walt Masters appeared in eight games as a pitcher in three seasons in the majors (1931 in Washington, 1937 with the Phillies and 1939 with the A's); his career won-lost record is 0-0. He also appeared in three seasons in the NFL with little effect (1936 with the Eagles, 1943 with the Cardinals and 1944 with the Cardinals-Steelers merged team). The record of the NFL teams on which he played was 1-31. The 1936 Eagles were the only one of the three teams to win a game.

10. Bert Kuczynski was 0-1 as a pitcher for the A's in 1943, and played end for two games with the Detroit Lions that year. He later played in two games with the 1946 Eagles. In his NFL career, he caught four passes for 13 yards and one touchdown.

 OVERTIME: *Uniform Number Question:* Intense linebacker Bill Romanowski wore 53 for the Eagles, 49ers, Broncos and Raiders, and won Super Bowls with the 49ers and Broncos.

QUIZ ANSWERS !!!!

SECTION VI
RECORDS

GAME RECORDS

1. Steve Van Buren gained 205 yards on 27 carries in a 34-17 win over the Steelers in Shibe Park on November 27, 1949. Van Buren did not score that day. Duce Staley ran for 201 yards in an opening-day, 41-14 victory over the Cowboys in 2000 known as the "Pickle Juice Game" for what the Eagles drank to avoid heat cramps.

2. Steve Van Buren was one, carrying 35 times for 174 yards in a 42-0 shellacking of the New York Bulldogs at Shibe Park on November 20, 1949. He scored twice. Heath Sherman was the other, carrying the ball 35 times for 124 yards in the "Body Bag Game" on November 12, 1990 against the Redskins, and again in October 6, 1991 against the Bucs. The 14-13 loss to the lowly Bucs was the infamous game that unprepared rookie Brad Goebel started, and Sherman's 35 carries only netted 89 yards that day.

3. End Joe Carter scored four times in the Eagles' most decisive victory of all time, 64-0 over the Cincinnati Reds on November 6, 1934. It was the Reds' last game in the NFL as they disbanded the next week. Clarence Peaks, Tommy McDonald, Ben Hawkins and Wilbert Montgomery have also scored four touchdowns in a game. Most recently, Irving Fryar caught four TDs on October 20, 1996 against Miami.

4. Greasy Neale, of course. The rumbling, ground-oriented offense of the 1940s Eagles was what Greasy wanted and he really got it on November 21, 1948 when the team gained 376 yards rushing, 171 by Steve Van Buren, in beating the Redskins 42-21 at Shibe Park. Van Buren scored a touchdown and intercepted a pass on defense.

5. All-time Eagle scoring leader Bobby Walston scored 25 points on October 17, 1954 at Griffith Stadium. He caught three of Adrian Burks' record seven touchdown passes that day and added seven extra points.

6. Would you believe Joe Kuharich? On November 7, 1965, the Eagles lost to the Browns 38-34 in Cleveland, yet outgained them 582 yards to 369. The Eagles had 352 yards passing and 230 rushing (182 by Timmy Brown) in a losing effort.

7. On October 2, 1989, Randall Cunningham attempted 62 passes in a 27-14 *Monday Night Football* loss to the Bears in Chicago. Cunningham broke Davey O'Brien's team mark of 60 attempts against the Redskins in 1940. Cunningham completed 32 passes for 401 yards.

8. Randall Cunningham. On September 17, 1989, Cunningham threw for 447 yards in a furious, late-comeback 42-37 victory over the Redskins in Washington. On that day, Cunningham broke Bobby Thomason's 36-year-old team record of 437 yards passing against the Giants on November 8, 1953.

9. Pete Liske threw six interceptions against the Cowboys in a 42-7 loss at the Vet on September 26, 1971. Herb Adderley had three of the picks himself. Liske equaled Bobby

Thomason's team mark set against the Cardinals in a 20-6 loss at Connie Mack Stadium on October 21, 1956.

10. Rich Kotite coached the Eagles when they racked up 191 penalty yards on 17 penalties against the Seahawks on December 13, 1992. The highest number of penalties came under Buddy Ryan with 19 in an October 2, 1988 game against Houston. The Eagles won both games.

 OVERTIME: *Uniform Number Question:* Ryan traded the back end of his 1989 draft to the Bears to allow him to move up in the third round and grab the active hitter Britt Hager.

Quiz Answers
SEASONAL RECORDS

1. It may be startling that the Eagles scored their most points in 2002, the year that Donovan McNabb missed the last six games with a broken ankle. Yet they scored 415 points that year with a fairly balanced offense for pass-happy Andy Reid in which Duce Staley gained over 1,000 yards on the ground. Still that team averaged 25.9 points per game, while the championship teams from 1948 and 1949 both exceeded 30 points a game. In 1948, the Eagles scored 376 points in 12 games for an average of 3 1.3. The following season they scored 364 points in 12 games for a 30.3 average.

2. The kicker for the back-to-back champs was guard Cliff Patton, who set a league record with 84 consecutive points after touchdown over three seasons that was exceeded by David Akers this decade. In 1948, he converted 50 of 50 extra points, and that is still a team record.

3. As expected, the answer is Steve Van Buren with 15 touchdowns rushing in 1945. He added two more on receptions and one on a kickoff return to total 18 touchdowns for a league-leading 108 points. The NFL touchdown record was 18 till Van Buren was tied by Jimmy Brown in 1958 and topped by Jim Taylor in 14 games in 1962.

4. Donovan McNabb's remarkable 31 touchdowns in 2004 fell one short of the team record held by Sonny Jurgensen with 32 in the 14-game season of 1961.

5. The year after Jurgensen threw 32 touchdowns against 24 interceptions, he dropped to 22 touchdowns against 26 interceptions. He would never exceed 19 interceptions for the rest of his career.

6. Keith Byars was used as an H-back as much as a regular runner because he was so good at catching the ball and was much more effective in gaining ground when he was out in the open rather than taking a handoff from scrimmage. He caught 81 balls in 1990. In 1992, he replaced the departed Keith Jackson as tight end for a season.

7. Bill Bradley had 11 interceptions in 1971 to lead the league and followed that with nine in 1972, another league-leading total. Only two other Eagles have ever intercepted nine passes in a season: Bibbles Bawel in 1955 and Don Burroughs in 1960.

8. Eric Allen picked off six passes in 1993 and returned four of them for touchdowns, scoring 24 points on defense.

9. Little Allen Rossum didn't always make the best decisions on punt returns, but he holds the team record for kickoff return yards with 1,367 in 1999. He was traded to the Packers the next season and replaced by the NFL's all-time leader in kick-return yardage, Brian Mitchell.

10. The NFL's all-time leader in kick-return yardage is also the NFL's all-time leader in punt-return yardage. Furthermore, Brian Mitchell holds the Eagles' seasonal mark for punt-return yards with 567 in 2002.

 OVERTIME: *Uniform Number Question:* 55 was worn by Maxie Baughan, who played six wonderful years in Philadelphia before falling out with Joe Kuharich and being traded to the Rams. Baughan called defensive signals for Los Angeles under George Allen, and Allen called the Baughan trade the best he ever made. Not for the Eagles.

═══ Quiz Answers 56 ═══
CAREER RECORDS

1. Ron Jaworski holds the team record with 175 touchdown passes. He blew by Norm Snead's previous career record of 111 in the strike season of 1982.

2. Tommy Thompson, the one-eyed quarterback of the 1948-49 champions, threw 100 interceptions in his Eagle career against 90 touchdowns. Norm Snead broke Thompson's career team interception record with 124, and Ron Jaworski topped that with 151.

3. Thomas "Swede" Hanson led the Eagles in rushing in each of their first four seasons and

finished second in the NFL in 1934 with 805 yards. His career total as an Eagle was 1,907. Steve Van Buren passed that in his fourth year of 1947.

4. Quarterback Adrian Burk punted 393 times in his Eagle career as he alternated at quarterback with Bobby Thomason. Neither could win the quarterback job for good since both were so inconsistent. Punting was frequently handled by a quarterback in those days, and both Norm Van Brocklin and King Hill punted for the team for many years. Second in Eagle punts is pure punter Sean Landeta with 376 punts through 2005.

5. Reggie White broke Greg Brown's record for sacks by an Eagle in his third year. Brown tallied 50.5 sacks in his career in Philadelphia; Reggie ended up with 124 sacks as an Eagle and 198 for his entire career. Of course, sacks were not counted till 1982, so the quarterback sacks of earlier sack masters like Norm Willey were not officially counted at all and those of stars like Dennis Harrison were not counted at the beginning of their careers.

6. Cunningham passed Ron Jaworski's 772 yards rushing as a quarterback in his third year, 1987, soon after Jaws left the team. In those years, Randall was desperately running for his life as the Eagle offensive line was mostly offensive to the fans. They surrendered a team-record 104 sacks in 1986 and 72 in 1987. Cunningham holds the NFL mark for yards rushing by a quarterback as well with 4,928 yards.

7. Harold Carmichael scored 79 touchdowns in his Eagle career. When he started, the 6'8" wide receiver was famous for crazy end-zone celebrations such as pretending he was shooting craps with the football and sweeping windmill spikes, but as he got older the celebrations calmed down.

8. In 1956, Bobby Walston became the Eagles' all-time leading scorer, passing Steve Van Buren's 464 points. Walston has now held the team scoring record for 50 years, and it will be another two years at least before David Akers may top the 881 points with which Walston finished.

9. Harold Carmichael played in 180 games in 13 seasons as an Eagle. Only Chuck Bednarik was an Eagle for more seasons. However, Bednarik's 14 seasons were shorter, so he only appeared in 169 games. Other long-tenured Eagles include Bucko Kilroy and Vic Sears with 13 seasons and Bobby Walston and Jerry Sisemore with 12.

10. Dick Vermeil passed Greasy Neale's 45 losses before he burned out and leads with 47 through 2005. Andy Reid will probably at least tie if not surpass Vermiel in 2006, though, because he goes into the season with 42 losses. The most losses by an Eagle coach with a losing record is 44 by Bert Bell because it is hard for a bad coach to get fired when he is also the owner of the team.

 OVERTIME: *Uniform Number Question:* 56 was worn by Buddy Ryan's middle linebacker Byron Evans, who decided it would behoove him to try the free-agent waters like so many of his former defensive teammates and turned down a rich contract extension in 1994.

ROOKIES

1. Don Looney, who had played with tailback Davey O'Brien at Texas Christian, caught 58 passes for 707 yards as a rookie in 1940 and led the league in receptions. He beat out perennial leader Don Hutson by 13 catches in one of only three seasons in Hutson's 11-year career that he did not lead the NFL in receptions. Looney had a short career in the NFL and an even shorter one in Philadelphia. In 1941, Looney went to Pittsburgh in the franchise trade and would play in only 13 games in two years, catching just 17 more passes.

2. Steve Van Buren was not only big and powerful, he was also fast. He led the league in punt-return average with 15.3 as a rookie and ran back both a punt and kickoff for touchdowns to go with the five he scored from scrimmage.

3. Correll Buckhalter with 586 yards in 2000. Surprisingly, it isn't either of the two greatest backs in team history, Steve Van Buren and Wilbert Montgomery. Van Buren was still recovering from appendicitis at the beginning of 1944, and so only carried the ball 80 times as a rookie. Montgomery spent his rookie year returning kicks and didn't get a chance to start until the last game of the season when he gained over 100 yards rushing against the Jets.

4. Diminutive Davey O'Brien, all 5'7" and 150 pounds of him, led the NFL with 1,324 yards passing in 1939. He threw six touchdowns and 17 interceptions on a team that finished 1-9-1. Fellow rookie Parker Hall of the Cleveland Rams was second with 1,227 yards passing that year. O'Brien only played for two years and only won two games in that time, but he was a big fan favorite because of his size and his "aw shucks" manner.

5. In 1949, the defending champs were joined by Chuck Bednarik, who got to play more and more as the year went on in a rotation with center Vic Lindskog and linebacker Alex Wojciechowicz. In 1950, Norm "Wild Man" Willey earned a spot at defensive end by the end of the season. In 1961, cornerback Irv Cross was forced into the starting lineup for the last five games of the year when Tom Brookshier broke his leg.

6. Tom Brookshier and Bibbles Bawel both had eight interceptions in their rookie seasons. Brookshier spent his next two years in the military and then returned in 1961 for six more Eagle seasons, but never had more than four picks in any other season and finished up with 20 for his career. Bawel also was called into the military for two years following his rookie campaign. However, he came back with a bang, nabbing nine picks in 1955. He only grabbed one interception in 1956 and dropped out of football.

7. Paul McFadden scored 116 points in 1984 on 30 field goals and 26 extra points. He would only score more than 100 points one other time in his six-year career in Philadelphia, New York and Atlanta. McFadden broke Tony Franklin's club rookie record of 105 points in 1979. Before Franklin, Bobby Walston's 94 points in 1951 was the record.

8. Bob Suffridge from Tennessee received All-Pro recognition as a rookie wearing what would become Chuck Bednarik's 60. Suffridge then served in World War II for four years. He returned to the Eagles wearing 75 for 1945 and then retired. He was later elected to the College Football Hall of Fame.

9. It was not Davey O'Brien who led the league in passing yards as a rookie. Bobby Hoying appeared in one game in 1996, so that must count as his rookie season, but in 1997, the first year he played, he passed for 1,573 yards. The answer is John Reaves, who threw for 1,508 yards along with seven touchdowns and 12 interceptions as he completed just 48% of his passes in 1972 as a rookie. He was horribly undercoached and overmatched, and his career went downhill from there. Donovan McNabb passed for just 948 yards as a rookie.

10. Bobby Walston caught 31 passes with eight for touchdowns in 1951. He scored 48 points with his hands and added 46 points with his toe to accumulate 94 points as a rookie. In only one other season would this tough, reliable receiver catch as many touchdowns: 1954 with 11 TDs.

 OVERTIME: *Uniform Number Question:* Linebacker Keith Adams is the son of 16-year Patriot defensive lineman Julius Adams.

QUIZ ANSWERS 58

AWARDS

1. Greasy Neale won Coach of the Year in 1948 with his first title, and Buck Shaw won it in 1960 with his championship. Dick Vermeil won in 1979 for turning around a moribund franchise, and Ray Rhodes won in 1995 for breathing fire into a tottering team. Andy Reid has won twice: once in 2000 for turning the franchise around and in 2002 for keeping the team on course despite losing his first- and second-string quarterbacks.

2. Greasy Neale was fired two years after winning the award by dropping to 6-6 in 1950. Rhodes was fired three years later when the team was in a death spiral. Shaw and Vermeil retired on their own, and Reid is still going.

3. Pete Retzlaff won the Bert Bell Award from the Philadelphia-based Maxwell Club in 1966, an honor never received by another tight end before or since. Pete did have his best season that year with 66 catches for 1,190 yards and 10 touchdowns, but he was third in

catches, and second in yards and touchdowns, while the team finished 5-9. Meanwhile, the first-place Browns featured Jim Brown's league-leading 1,544 yards and 21 TDs. The second-place Colts were led by Johnny Unitas' 2,530 yards and 23 touchdowns. John Brodie on the 49ers threw for 3,112 yards and 30 TDs, while Bears rookie runner Gale Sayers accumulated 2,272 all-purpose yards and a league-leading 22 touchdowns.

4. All quarterbacks. Norm Van Brocklin won a league MVP award for leading the improbable 1960 Eagles to the title. Ron Jaworski won it in 1980 for leading the Eagles to the Super Bowl. Randall Cunningham won it in 1988 and 1990 for being the "Ultimate Weapon." Randall won it one more time in 1998 with the Vikings.

5. Reggie White, of course, in 1987 with 21 sacks and 1991 with 15 sacks on probably the best defense in football.

6. Again all quarterbacks. Roman Gabriel won Comeback Player of the Year in 1973, his first year with the Eagles, after a subpar last season with the Rams. Jim McMahon, who replaced the injured Randall Cunningham in 1991, for coming back to life after a three-year decline into the second string. Randall himself the following year for coming back from his knee injury to again lead the Eagles to the playoffs and even win a playoff game.

7. Bert Bell gave 5'7" tailback Davey O'Brien a plaque with this inscription after the last game in his two-year career, a game in which he set NFL records for pass attempts, completions and yards. Of course, that day he lost for the 19th time in 22 Eagle games.

8. Chuck Bednarik was named to an All-Pro team 10 times in 14 seasons. Second to Bednarik are Pete Pihos and Al Wistert with eight apiece.

9. Again the answer is Chuck Bednarik—this time with eight. Right behind Chuck is Reggie White with seven, and that's seven straight selections. Reggie set an NFL mark by being named to the Pro Bowl 13 years in a row because he was named all six of his years in Green Bay.

10. Bill Romanowski won four Super Bowl rings, two in San Francisco and two in Denver. Art Monk and Guy McIntyre each won three Super Bowl rings, in Washington and San Francisco, respectively. For pre-Super Bowl players, both Abe Gibron with the Browns and Stan Campbell with the Lions and Eagles played on three NFL championship teams. They were both guards. Jack Myers, a backup fullback and linebacker with the 1948-49 Eagle champs, won a third championship as a member of the Rams in 1951. He was the only player who was on two Eagle championship teams that ever won anything anywhere else.

 OVERTIME: *Uniform Number Question:* Mel Tom wore 58 at first because he was drafted in the sixth round as a linebacker in 1966 before being converted to defensive end. He didn't shift to 99 till his fifth season, 1971, when he became the second Eagle to wear a number in the 90s.

HONOR ROLL

1. In 1995, the Eagles honored longtime Eagles executive Jim Gallagher. The following year, the late Jerome Brown was added. After a three-year gap, the Eagles honored trainer Otho Davis and the 1948 and 1949 championship teams in 1999. There have been no additions in this century. Instead of doing a blanket, one-shot honor for the back-to-back champs, the Eagles could have been honoring some of the unsung heroes from those great teams like Al Wistert, Bucko Kilroy, Vic Sears, Tommy Thompson, Jack Ferrante, Bosh Pritchard, Russ Craft, Joe Muha and Vic Lindskog before they are all gone.

2. Norm Van Brocklin, Sonny Jurgensen and Ron Jaworski, although only Jaworski was a starter for more than three seasons in Philadelphia. Van Brocklin supplied the franchise with a title, but Jurgensen unfortunately had most of his Hall of Fame career in Washington.

3. Chuck Bednarik and Alex Wojciechowicz, who both spent more time at linebacker, and Jim Ringo, who spent most of his Hall of Fame career in Green Bay.

4. Kuharich obtained Jim Ringo and Ollie Matson in two of his many trades; Matson was an old favorite of Joe's from the days when Joe coached him in college and with the Cardinals. Pete Retzlaff and Timmy Brown were already here when Joe arrived, and Brown in particular never got along with Kuharich and his "no stars" policy.

5. Chuck Bednarik played the longest for the Eagles, but executive Jim Gallagher arrived in the team's front office in 1949 when Bednarik was a rookie and didn't retire till 1995. In fact, Gallagher still is very active with the Eagles' alumni organization.

6. Ollie Matson spent the last three seasons of his 14-year Hall of Fame career in Philadelphia accumulating the last 600 yards of his 5,100 yards rushing total.

7. Bert Bell, who is in the Hall of Fame as an owner and commissioner, not as a coach; Hall of Famer Greasy Neale; and Dick Vermeil.

8. Bookends for nine years from 1975 to 1983, Jerry Sisemore and Stan Walters are arguably the greatest set of tackles the Eagles have ever had. Sisemore had the longer career, playing from 1973 to 1984.

9. Hall of Famers Bill Hewitt, Pete Pihos and Tommy McDonald, and All-Pros Pete Retzlaff, Harold Carmichael and Mike Quick.

10. 1960 and 1980 are tied. Five from the 1948-49 champs are honored: Bednarik, Pihos, Van Buren, Wojciechowicz and Neale. Seven are honored from the 1960 champs: Bednarik, Tom Brookshier, Tim Brown, Sonny Jurgensen, Tommy McDonald, Pete Rezlaff and Norm Van Brocklin. Seven are honored from the 1980 Super Bowl team, too: Bill Bergey, Harold Carmichael, Ron Jaworski, Wilbert Montgomery, Jerry Sisemore, Stan Walters and Dick Vermeil.

OVERTIME: *Uniform Number Question:* North Catholic's Mike Evans, who was the team's center in between Jim Ringo and Guy Morriss. Evans lost his starting job when he came down with the flu in 1973, giving rookie guard Guy Morriss an opening.

QUIZ ANSWERS
THE HALL OF FAME

1. Bert Bell was a charter member of the Hall of Fame in 1963, but had passed away in 1959. Bill Hewitt was inducted in 1971. He is remembered as being especially effective in rushing the passer and for being among the last players in the league to go without a helmet. When he returned to play with the Steagles in 1943 after a four-year absence, he wore a helmet for the first time. He died in a car accident on Bethlehem Pike in 1947.

2. Deep threat receiver James Lofton appeared in nine games with Philadelphia at the tail end of his career in 1993 and caught 13 passes for Rich Kotite's offense. Before Lofton was inducted in 2003, this distinction went to Mike Ditka, who lasted two years (just 20 games) as an Eagle under Joe Kuharich, whom he hated, and caught 39 passes for four touchdowns.

3. Neale presented two of his star Eagle linebackers: Chuck Bednarik in 1967 and Alex Wojciechowicz. Wojie is not listed as a primary Eagle by the Hall of Fame since he played five years in Philly and eight in Detroit, but he was a rugged defender for the glory years of Neale's team. He made the Hall of Fame despite receiving All-Pro recognition only in his second season.

4. Neale had Bednarik introduce him in 1969, even though Chuck played for Greasy for only two seasons, and Neale was a coach who had a great preference for veterans. However, he and Neale seemed to have a special bond. Neale had even invited the rookie into his regular pinochle game with Duke Maronic and Jack Ferrante in 1949.

5. Van Buren surpassed Hinkle's 3,860 yards rushing in the 1949 opener to become the NFL's all-time leading rusher.

6. Ray Didinger is a local icon and longtime fixture in covering the Eagles and the NFL for the Philadelphia *Bulletin* and *Daily News* and then NFL Films, WIP radio and Comcast Sportsnet TV. Didinger grew up admiring the pluck and talent of McDonald and, as a

Hall of Fame selector, argued for his candidacy for many years. When Tommy finally was inducted in 1998, he chose Didinger to introduce him in a classy gesture.

7. Steve Van Buren, Pete Pihos and Chuck Bednarik played eight, nine and 14 years in the NFL, respectively, and none of them played anywhere but Philadelphia. In addition, Greasy Neale coached only the Eagles.

8. All five from those greatest of all Eagle teams were inducted in a six-year period: Steve Van Buren in 1965, Chuck Bednarik in 1967, Alex Wojciechowicz in 1968, Greasy Neale in 1969 and end Pete Pihos in 1970. All but Bednarik were involved with both championship seasons. It is a shame that Al Wistert and Bucko Kilroy are not in Canton with them.

9. These four Hall of Famers were inducted over a 30-year period: Bednarik was inducted in 1967; Norm Van Brocklin went in 1971; Sonny Jurgensen, who was a mere backup in 1960, was inducted in 1983, and Tommy McDonald in 1998. It is unlikely that anyone else from that team will be selected, although one could argue for Pete Retzlaff.

10. The coach, Bert Bell, was also an owner, but he was not a great college player. The center was Jim Ringo from Syracuse. The runner was Steve Van Buren of LSU, who spent most of his college career in the shadows, as did the passer Sonny Jurgensen of Duke. The two receivers were Bill Hewitt of Michigan and James Lofton of Stanford. All were more memorable as pros than as undergraduates.

 OVERTIME: *Uniform Number Question:* Guard Don Weedon from Texas, who served in World War II and played one game for the Eagles in 1947. The jersey barely needed to be washed for Chuck to slip it on in 1949.

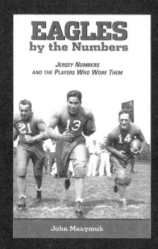